# AN INSIDER'S
# AUCTIONS

# AN INSIDER'S GUIDE TO
# AUCTIONS

# SYLVIA AUERBACH

toExcel

San Jose  New York  Lincoln  Shanghai

# An Insider's Guide to Auctions

Published by toExcel

For information address:
toExcel
165 West 95th Street, Suite B-N
New York, NY  10025
www.toExcel.com

ISBN: 1-58348-321-7

LCCN: 99-62830

Printed in the United States of America

*Photographs by Arley Bondarin*

*Book design by Leslie Bauman*

*Grateful acknowledgement is given to Crown Publishers for their permission to reproduce line illustrations from the 1902 Edition of The Sears, Roebuck Catalogue.*

# CONTENTS

BLACKWOOD &CO. AUCTION
VFW. Rte. 1A IPSWICH

AUGUST 14TH
THURSDAY
EVENING 6:30 P.M.

# PART ONE

# THE AUCTION GAME

# 1     AUCTIONS: COME AS YOU ARE

Welcome to the blooming, booming world of the auction. No need for a formal invitation—come as you are, whether you're wearing blue jeans and a T-shirt, a business suit (male or female variety), a designer dress and sable coat, a Brooks Brothers suit and Gucci loafers. Come in a bus, the subway, your station wagon, van, subcompact, big four-door gas guzzler, even your limousine. Come to observe, furnish your home, add to your collection of whatever you collect, acquire a fine painting, find a rare antique—or even a perfect little table to eat on while you're watching television. But do come to the auction. Where else can shopping be a combination of adventure, test of wills, history lesson, and antique show, and best of all, a source of bargains and good solid finds? In the words of one devotee who has worked in the auction business at everything from moving heavy furniture to appraising fine art in Park Avenue penthouses, the auction is "the greatest game ever invented for grownups."

*The New Auction Boom*

"The action's at the auction" is the current popular phrase—and it's true. And for good reason. More and more newcomers are joining the ranks of veteran auction-goers because they've discovered that the auction is one place that offers the possibility of overcoming some of the afflictions of today's marketplace: high prices, inflation, shoddy workmanship, mass-produced items. More than that, the auction itself is a unique experience, offering, in addition to the merchandise: *fun* (the auctioneers and their helpers are often stand-up comics as they play to the crowd); *drama* (millionaires bidding against each other in a hushed gallery as a nod of the head or a raise of the eyebrows means "I'll go another $10,000"); *a glimpse of other people's lives* (as estates go on the block, prominent families or people around the corner). Auctions offer the chance to satisfy the urge to own something unique, or uncommon, or, to find some treasure in a carton of junk, to learn something about our country's history at sales of early Americana, to linger over masterpieces formerly in private collections, or to engage in some sociability after a long day's work.

Some people love the gambling aspect of auctions; taking a chance by bidding on boxes full of assorted books, brass, odds and ends, jewelry, or tools, and possibly finding something of real value. I share that feeling—maybe all auction-goers do, to a degree. A friend and I split the $2 cost of a carton of clothes at a little country auction. He took out a serviceable, down-to-the-floor raincoat to keep in his van for unexpected showers; I kept a purple wool stole; and we just threw away the rest!

*12*

According to one psychoanalyst, behind this gambling motive is a slightly darker impulse, a little bit of larceny, the hope that you'll get something worth much more than the sum you paid for it. Looking on the bright side, we might call it the lure of Lady Luck, the fairy-tale dream that you'll spend $5 and get something that's really worth thousands. Don't think that only amateurs have this dream. Dealers, too, when they're at an auction, will buy something whose value they're not sure of, in the hopes that they'll be lucky and be able to sell it at another auction for a high profit.

People also go to auctions to offer themselves a bit of consolation, says another psychologist. "I can't afford something new, but maybe I can find something I *can* afford." All of us cherish the thought that once in a while we can defy the gods and escape the usual confines of our lives; the auction is an exciting—and safe—place to do it.

In this panoply of attractions, the main attraction is

still the goods being auctioned off—and the promise they hold of satisfying some human need, whether it's utilitarian, aesthetic, or decorative. I once sat next to a young actor in a Greenwich Village auction house and watched him, in less than an hour and for about $300, get enough furniture in good condition to comfortably and attractively furnish a one-bedroom apartment. People attend auctions for that most ancient of human motives, to find a true bargain, something of value either to keep or, perhaps, to enjoy only for a time and then sell in the future, at a fine profit.

What's auctioned off? A more easily answered question might be, what isn't? From Z to A, the range is nothing short of mind-boggling. Here is just a random sample of some goods that were on the auction block in recent months. They may not be the sort of thing you and I would be interested in, but they do give you some idea of the scope of the auction world. Just consider these: A U.S. government yacht, the *Sequoia,* the site of historic meetings between Roosevelt and Churchill, Lyndon Johnson and the British royal family, and Nixon, Kissinger and the Russian Communist leaders Leonid Brezhnev and Andrei Gromyko; a Stradivarius violin (withdrawn by its owner who wasn't satisfied with the $95,000 bid); a bottle of 1806 Chateau Lafite-Rothschild wine which, at $28,000, came to about $500 per swallow; walking sticks (*the* thing in Paris); rare plants, from three inches to thirty feet in height; monsters that formerly enchanted or frightened children of all ages in the fun house at the Steel Pier in Atlantic City; "lipographs"—kisses on postcards (Muhammed Ali, $1,160; Marlene Dietrich, $1,200; Mick Jagger, $1,600); coin-operated gambling machines; autographs (Elvis Presley's signature on a napkin from the Las Vegas Riviera Hotel brought $2,700); antique cars (a 1936 Mercedes roadster sold for $400,000 and a 1955 Ford Thunderbird brought $17,000).

*14*

The news media always have stories about such items at an auction, and it is fun to read about them, to go and see them avidly bid for. But fun aside, the truth is that they are only a very small part of the real business of auctions, which is to provide an instant and important marketplace for all kinds of useful, sometimes ordinary, often basic, not-at-all exotic goods.

Consider, for instance, these major auction fields in which millions of dollars are continuously being spent: automobiles, both new and vintage; all kinds of marine equipment, including boats; tobacco; horses; tea; coffee; real estate, including land, residential, industrial and commercial; coins; stamps; store fixtures; all kinds of government equipment; "lost, strayed and stolen merchandise" from police departments.

Money itself is auctioned. Uncle Sam borrows billions from us at regular auctions of U.S. Treasury Bills, and the interest they pay is a bellwether of the interest rates charged on other borrowings. (For that matter, the stock market is nothing more than a continuous auction of the assets of corporations.) The meat on our tables comes to us by way of cattle auctions. Open-the-gate-and-walk-'em-in auctioneers do business in the billions and can be connoisseurs of purebred animals no less expert than the connoisseurs in the major fine-arts auction houses. (Furthermore, bulls are often sold with a "performance guarantee," a satisfactory semen test, which is more than you get when buying stocks!)

The list is endless, without even mentioning the auctions you and I are most likely to go to—furniture, rugs, household things, estate sales—because the auction method offers some unique advantages: a fast disposal of property through public competition, while keeping to a minimum the costs of storage, promotion, and display. It may have been these very advantages that prompted the Romans to use auctions (the Latin word *auctio* means, literally, "an increasing") to dispose of their property.

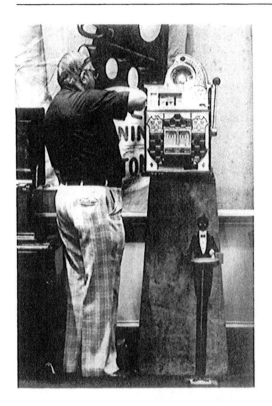 

*A Short History of Auctions*

It's not known whether it was the Romans who brought auctions to the British Isles, but the British have traditionally used auctions to sell real estate, art, furniture and household goods. When Charles I was executed in 1649, his collection of paintings, sold on the block, glutted the art market and kept it depressed for almost a century. The fabulous art collection of the royal Stuart family was auctioned at prices, say historians, that had not been achieved since Roman times. The British tradition of auctions resulted not only in the rise of the great London auction houses, Christie's and Sotheby's, but also of their great American offspring.

The settlers in the New World brought the tradition of

## In More Ways Than One, Roman Auctions Were Historic!

*Various historians tell us that Roman auctions were not too different from the auctions we have today. James Bough, in his book* Auction!, *says that the infamous Roman emperor Caligula put about $5 million worth of his family's furniture and ornaments on the block to help cover his debts. A Roman named Apponius went to the sale and dozed off. The auctioneer took his nodding head as a signal that he was bidding—and Apponius was surprised, when he woke up, to find that he was the new owner of Caligula's goods. (Could this story be the origin of the idea that you have to watch your movements at an auction if you don't want to find that you've unwittingly bought something?)*

*Here's another good auction story from the Roman period. In the first century A.D., the Praetorian guard beheaded the emperor Pertinax, and then discovered that no one was willing to take over the job. So they decided to auction off the empire to the highest bidder, which turned out to be a patriotic and wealthy Roman, Didius, who bid after he failed to rally his countrymen against the Praetorians. He was crowned emperor, but not for long. Armies in the field hastened back to Rome. A general, Severus, arrived first and took control of the Senate, the population, and the Praetorians—who quickly deserted Didius (but kept his money). Unlucky Didius was beheaded, and his head, mounted on a spear, was carried through the streets where it could be mocked and spat upon, perhaps history's unluckiest successful bidder!*

auctions with them. Indeed, when supply ships from England and Holland landed, the captains quickly disposed of their cargo through auctions. The earliest recorded sale of an auction in the colonies was in 1662; Boston, Philadelphia, and New York were the primary auction cities in the early days. Major art sales and antique and furniture auctions didn't take place until the middle of the nineteenth century, but from that time on, sales records were made and broken. In the era before the 1929 Depression, art and antique collections, and sometimes the mansions on Fifth Avenue that housed them, sold for record-breaking millions of dollars. As happens today, fortunate owners sold some of their collections for three, four, or more times the original price.

Wars, politics, economics, and real needs—plus styles, whims, and fads—fueled the auction market and kept prices fluctuating. The Depression of the 1930s kept auction prices low and important collections off the market. (Note that word *important,* by the way—it's a favorite term of auctioneers. It usually shows up at least once in any auction announcement, whether it's a single mimeographed sheet announcing a country auction or a glossy, elegant catalog from one of New York's glossy, elegant auction houses.) Prices picked up slowly after the Depression, and every decade since has had its share of new records. But few of these records have matched the peaks of the last decade, particularly its last few years, when sales fueled what one London dealer called "public insanity." Which brings us to the current auction boom.

### What's Behind the Boom

Today the auction market is literally in the billions of dollars annually. Observers of the field (many with a vested interest) offer a variety of reasons for this incredible boom. Here in no special order are the major ones.

• National interest in antiques got a tremendous boost when First Lady Jacqueline Kennedy refurbished the White House with pieces from the past. You may remember the televised tours of the White House that were seen by a huge national audience.

• The Bicentennial celebrations all around the country gave us a fresh look at colonial America, including its furniture, decorative objects, and household utensils. We

enjoyed seeing the many exhibits, reading the many stories, and developed a wider awareness of and a new pride in our country's past.

• There is a continually growing interest in hand-crafted goods, as a cultural revolt against the "plastic" society and mass production. As a result, in addition to generating new artists and hobbyists, this interest has stimulated a desire for the handcrafted objects of the past.

• The *Roots* phenomenon: this revival of interest in our various ethnic backgrounds invariably leads us, again, to the past and to the arts that expressed those backgrounds.

• A growing well-educated middle and upper middle class, with an interest in art from college courses, travel,

*19*

and reading—and a desire to participate in the arts by collecting—is confident enough to bypass dealers and make its own choices at auctions. One estimate indicates that private collectors now buy about half of all the art in the major auction sales, in contrast to ten years ago when dealers were the major buyers.

• Inflation. As the buying power of the dollar has declined, and along with it the value of such money investments as stocks, bonds, and bank accounts, there's been a corresponding rise in the desire to invest in material objects (tangibles, to use the Wall Street jargon) that have appreciated in value: art, antiques, gold, coins, jewelry, stamps, paintings, decorative objects.

• Nostalgia for the time when life was supposedly better leads people to want to buy some of that past. Presumably owning things from the past is somehow a promise that the better times will return. (Is it self-delusion? People who collect Depression glass certainly forget or are too young to remember the desperation of the Depression years, when the stock market crashed and twelve million people were unemployed.)

• The one-way trade from England and the European continent. Because of high taxes and a dearth of servants, it has become more and more difficult for wealthy Europeans to maintain their huge estates and castles. They've taken to exporting their belief that "people of means" invest in antiques and fine art—and by some chance their own antiques and fine art are now available for Americans to buy at auctions at very modern high prices. Interestingly enough, as this one-way trade has led to the expansion of the American auction market, it in turn has become more and more of a world market, with people from all over the world buying at American auctions—not only in New York but also at major auction sales all around the country.

• And, last in the list, one slightly offbeat explanation: "hot money." One executive of a major auction house explains that in every country, certain amounts and

## Some Auctions Are Endurance Contests

*In 1970, when Metro Goldwyn Mayer wanted to dispose of a forty-three-year accumulation of movie memorabilia, they held an auction right on the studio grounds in Hollywood. It was as much an endurance contest as an auction. For eighteen days, in heat that never went below 90°, antique dealers, plus owners of restaurants, apartment houses, and boutiques—middle-aged entrepreneurs who could remember the movies whose artifacts they were buying—tramped around from lot to lot with the auctioneer.*

*MGM expected movie stars to come and buy, but only Debbie Reynolds showed up regularly. She wanted to start a Hollywood Hall of Fame, but received no support from the movie community. So she spent $100,000 of her own money (borrowed from a bank) to buy furniture, props, and costumes from, among other movies, one of Judy Garland's first triumphs, Meet Me in St. Louis.*

*Other buyers bought various items from the* Wizard of Oz, *in which Judy starred as Dorothy. The wicked witch's hat brought $450; the wizard's suit, $650. Dorothy's magic slippers went for $15,000 to a "cold-eyed attorney" (in the words of* The New York Times), *who was acting as agent for a local millionaire. But not everyone had cold eyes. A doctor from West Covina bought the cowardly lion's shabby suit. He said he had seen the* Wizard of Oz *when he was five years old, and that the movie had continued to "haunt" him through the years. "The costume isn't an investment," he said. "No one will ever wear the costume again."*

sources of money aren't "mentioned" to the tax collectors and aren't left sitting in a bank (not even a Swiss bank). So owners of this "hot money" (received for various introductions, business deals, contract awards) use it to buy collectibles.

Will the trend to buying at auction continue? You'd

better believe it. All the factors that led to the trend in the first place are still with us, and show no signs of diminishing. Certainly the recent presidential election confirmed the swing toward conservatism and the feeling that the past was better. Inflation is still with us, and investment advisory services are still touting the fact that tangibles are increasing in value even as the dollar continues to decline. (Cheery note: the minerals in the human body are now worth $7.28 compared to 98¢ at the beginning of the seventies.)

*Getting the Auction Bug*

Quite apart from all this, the auction business itself has become big business. It has geared itself to continue,

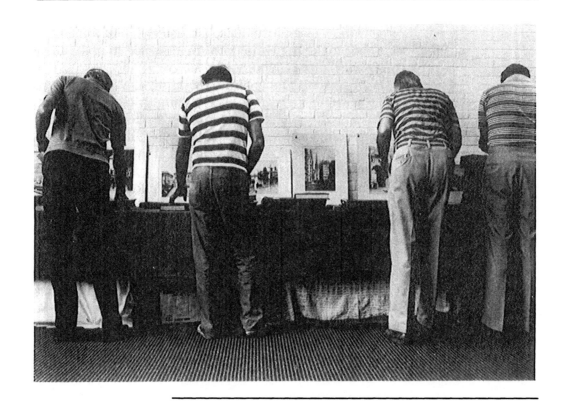

to widen its scope and accommodate its own growing market, and thereby to make the market grow. The old images of auctions—that there are only two kinds: the very la-di-da for the very rich, and the somewhat sleazy for the unsuspecting tourist—are being blown away in a whirlwind of carefully planned publicity on television and radio, in newsmagazines, in newsletters and newspapers catering to the auction-goer, and through a major expansion of the auction houses themselves.

The most interesting aspect of this expansion is that it's frankly aimed at the middle-level market. There are more Saturday, Sunday, and evening hours for the on-the-job nine-to-five middle class; more ads emphasizing that most items sell at auction for "under $1,000" or that "the average price at auction is $300"; and more free appraisal days to find the merchandise to sell at auction—and, not incidentally, to encourage people to make their first visit to an auction house.

It all adds up to a gigantic recycling movement, possibly the world's greatest. The timing is certainly propitious. For the smart buyer, auctions offer many of the elements that any sensible acquisition offers: satisfaction of a need (as the economists put it) at the right time and at the right price.

To which I will add the right article for the right purpose to the right customer. Many people who have never gone to an auction think only art and antiques are sold there—and that they are beyond the reach of "ordinary people." This attitude has been fostered by the general news media, which report only the main events, those record-breaking sales. Yes, high-priced art and antiques are a part of the auction world—but only a part. The other part of the auction world, the main part, is the continuous buying and selling of just about all the things we need to live with, from the utilitarian to the aesthetic: rugs, dishes, silverware, television sets, pots and pans, toys, costume jewelry, and so on, including good—but not masterpiece—art and antiques at affordable prices for the knowledgeable buyer.

Plus, the excitement of getting a real buy, the fun of remembering and telling about it afterward, and the possibility of having your purchase increase in value—though you may never want to part with it.

This is not to say that buying at auction is without hazards. Not all auction buys are good buys; some things are never worth a penny more than the price they sold for. Buying at auction is different than buying at a store; the knowledgeable customer must learn to deal with the differences and make them work to his or her advantage by learning the basics: examining, comparing, bidding, paying, transporting, and acquiring the tools of the trade—knowing when to wave your hand, and when to sit on it to resist temptation.

The purpose of this book is to make you knowledgeable as you have the fun of exploring the auction world. It is not a book about how to buy inordinately expensive antiques or art, or how to invest in tangibles; these are topics that are extensively covered in an infinite number of other sources. It is a guide to the basics of buying and selling in today's auction world. Once you learn these basics, you can apply them and adapt them to your dealings with any auction house, from the posh to the plebeian. You will be able to take advantage of the opportunities the auction world offers, without being caught unprepared; to acquire your heart's desire without losing your head or ruining your budget; to make sensible choices; and to separate the good from the shoddy, whether it's called junque or junk.

As we discuss the details of auction buying (and later on, auction selling), you'll get some behind-the-scenes glimpses of the people in the auction world, both customers and auctioneers. If you're a newcomer, you'll develop what psychologists call an "entering repertoire"; if you've been around but want to learn more, you'll sharpen your skills and become even more knowledgeable. In either case, the book will, I hope, help you avoid the pitfalls and savor the excitement, diversity, drama and, most important, the good buys.

# 2 THE GREAT AUCTION MARKETPLACE

Say "auction" to people and you get some very surprising reactions.

"You must go to all those big auctions," I say to my friend Anne, "those glamorous auctions at Sotheby's and Christie's." I know Anne is knowledgeable about antiques both because her mother owned an antique shop and because she herself is a collector of antique jewelry.

"Oh no," she says. "I'm much too intimidated."

Intimidated? A very successful public relations professional who is not intimidated by her clients, best-selling authors, nor by the people she promotes them to, those tough television and radio producers—intimidated by auctions?

But Anne is not alone.

"I know graduates of Harvard," says an executive of a

27

major auction house, "who would love to come to auctions, but are afraid they won't know how to act, or bid, or judge values—so they don't come."

"I've gone past that auction house dozens of times," says the professional photographer, "but I've never ventured in. It looks too dark and mysterious, somehow. It reminds me of those stories I've heard about Atlantic City auctions, where there are shills in the audience and people get taken."

"No, I just take people to that estate auction," says the cab driver, "but I don't go. I'm afraid if I coughed, I'd be buying something."

Unwarranted feelings, all of these, but fears and beliefs that keep people away from auctions, especially the big-name ones.

So before we go on to talk about the skills that will help you become a savvy auction-goer, let me give you a quick tour of the auction world. We'll look at the kind of marketplace it is, its many layers, and the characteristics of its leading fixture, the auctioneer. You'll quickly realize that there's no need to be intimidated.

## Department Store Versus Auction Gallery

One factor that may intimidate you is that buying an item at auction isn't like buying it at a place you're much more familiar with: a department store. There, the steps of the transaction are clear-cut, especially because you've been through them so many times. The transaction at an auction is unknown and, to a newcomer, seems somewhat obscure—but only in the beginning. Let's look at buying something in these two different places, so you can make your own comparison.

For an (oversimplified) example, let's take a hall mirror and consider how you might go about buying it at a department store. You decide to shop for it on your lunch hour, and you leave promptly at noon. You head for the store's mirror department, and examine the prices on the mirrors you like. Needless to say, the one you like the best costs more than you can afford. So, you compromise. You pick your second-best choice at the price marked. You'd like to take the mirror home with you; it's not too big a package. But you're planning to pick up a sandwich to eat at your desk, and you've already stayed about half an hour beyond your usual lunch time, so you decide to have it sent. You charge the mirror on your credit card and know you won't have to pay for it until the bill comes, in about a month.

When the mirror is delivered, you discover a small scratch on the frame. You complain to the store, and after some complaining on their part, they offer to replace it with a new mirror, or to return your money. Some stores will even pick up the damaged mirror and deliver the new one, at little or no charge.

Compare this to buying at auction. First of all, the price isn't fixed. It evolves, while you participate in setting the price by bidding. Second, what you are buying is something that's been used; it's not fresh off the assembly line. Third, you buy everything "as is." If, later on, you discover a scratch you hadn't noticed before, too bad. *You* must fix it or decide to live with it. Fourth, you usually pay immediately for what you've bought, most often with cash or traveler's checks (unless you've already established a credit rating with the auction house). Fifth, you are responsible for taking your purchase with you, or making your own delivery arrangements.

The bidding part sounds exciting—right? But the other parts? A little scary? A little difficult? Maybe. But don't decide until you consider the other special features of the auction marketplace, and see if, after all, it doesn't offer the kind of shopping experience that would fit very well into your lifestyle and your pocketbook.

"No set price" means the opportunity to set your own price, very often a bargain price, sometimes a terrific bargain price. Buying "as is"? You can examine the

goods beforehand, for as long as you like and as carefully as you like—as any smart auction-goer does (more about this in later chapters). With a little savvy, you're not likely to be unpleasantly surprised. In fact, there's an equal or greater chance that you'll be *pleasantly* surprised. Furthermore, what you buy is often something unusual or handsome or different—a hall mirror, for example, with the kind of carved walnut frame that's not made any more. For the price of a store-bought, mass-produced mirror, you have acquired something special which, had you not bought it at auction, would have been quite beyond your budget.

Finally, buying at a department store is a cut-and-dried transaction. At an auction, buying is part theater, and you're one of the actors or actresses. Auctions are exciting even if you're just a spectator, but especially if

you're part of the action. They offer a range of opportunities more interesting, varied, unusual, sometimes even zany, than the usual shopping mall or department store. And you don't have to be a millionaire, or even have a six-figure income, to be an auction buff.

### The Many-Layered Auction World

Now let's take a look at that range of opportunities. For simplicity's sake, let's group the auctions into three categories, from the most prestigious to the least. But don't let this grouping mislead you. If a small country auction ranks at the low end of the prestige scale, it sometimes compensates by offering the best buys. Low prestige doesn't necessarily mean junk—and many veteran auction-goers and dealers who also shop at the top know it. Prestige usually means quality—but not necessarily top quality for every item.

Let's start our tour of the auction world at the glamorous top, with the prestigious New York auction houses. Some of them are descendants of centuries-old English houses, and are now themselves parents and grandparents to more and more branches around the country, as the interest in auctions spreads. In their headquarters on Manhattan's elegant Upper East Side, they auction off the finest jewels, rarest antiques, most famous paintings, most sought-after *objets de vertu* (which can be roughly translated as a hodgepodge of bric-a-brac, some beautiful, some merely old or odd) to an equally hodgepodge audience. The standbys of the audience are the antique dealers, museum curators, millionaires with their current wives or mistresses, socialites, and more ordinary well-to-do mortals. This last includes most of us, and don't think the big auction houses aren't open to middle-income people. As the editor of *The Official Sotheby Parke Bernet Price Guide to Antiques and Decorative Arts* notes (the book was published in 1980): "Approximately 80 percent of all the objects sold by Sotheby's in the United States have fetched under $1000; approximately 60 percent of these fetched under $500."

As New York City becomes more and more international, and more and more a center for the international art world, the audience standbys are being joined by their counterparts from England, the Continent, Asia, the Middle East, and South America, depending (usually) on what objects and rarities are being auctioned. When Russian icons were auctioned at Christie's, for instance, the sounds of the Russian language mingled with the more customary sounds of French, German and Spanish, to say nothing of the upper-class English accents.

Japanese has always been a fairly commonplace language on the West Coast auction scene, because of the indigenous Japanese population. But now it is heard

## The Winning Tickets

*Many price records are made and broken at posh auction houses during "admission-by-ticket-only" special auctions that are highly publicized social events. Who gets tickets? Dealers, museum curators, and art gallery owners, plus a range of potential customers who are considered sufficiently knowledgeable, collection-minded and, above all, rich enough to be interested in the auctioneer's ware—in the future if not that evening. These people are also cultivated because their own collections might someday—because of death, divorce, boredom, or the opportunity for income-tax benefits—be consigned to the auction house that invited them to the auction. (In May 1980, Henry Ford's superb collection of French Impressionist paintings was sold for $18,390,000, to help pay for the divorce settlement with his second wife.)*

*The fortunate ticket holders line up outside the doors in a well-bred crush until it's time for the auction and the doors are finally opened. Some very well known customers are personally led to choice seats in the main auction gallery by chic women staff members; others find their own seats. Latecomers and less well known customers have to settle for seats in subsidiary rooms where they watch the auction on in-house video screens.*

*As for the fourth estate—the working press—it's standing room only.*

more and more at New York auctions, as the overseas Japanese build their collections of Western art and as private Japanese collectors indulge their tastes for Western musical instruments. (Conversely, Japanese swords, many of them brought back by veterans of World War II in the Pacific, are best-sellers at American auctions.) These days, in fact, when unusual collections are auctioned at one of New York's major galleries, the presale exhibitions—filled with dealers carrying attaché cases,

men in business suits, and high-fashion women—sometimes look like a scene in the waiting room of one of the world's big international airports.

More and more now, these big houses are organizing auctions around one or another type of item so as to appeal to specialized audiences: for example, European, Latin American, or modern art; or silver, clocks, toys, prints, photographs, or vintage clothing; or that all-encompassing category covering a multitude of fads if not sins, the "collectibles." These auctions are promoted to attract a whole new class of auction-goers: the younger, professional, high-income group who are being assiduously cultivated with the promise of getting in at the start of a trend in one of these specialized fields.

So much for the fashionable top. At the other end of the spectrum is the small country auction, typically held

in an old barn or plain cinderblock building, on a Sunday afternoon or on a weekday or Friday evening about 7:00. The floors are bare, seating is on folding chairs or wooden benches, and everyone expects to swelter in the summer (no air-conditioning) and to stay bundled up in the winter, unless they're sitting near one of the heaters. Advertising, if any, is a mimeographed flyer, and on sale can be anything from a "knick-knack" shelf to a 1965 Minneapolis Moline 45 tractor with power steering. In between there are pieces of furniture, pictures, dishes, tools, bedspreads, hand-crocheted doilies, toys, and on and on—all the things left behind by death, long distance moves, changes in plans, successes and failures. No designer dresses or custom-tailored suits, sterling silver cufflinks or stylish hairdos among the buyers here. The audience is in jeans or cotton skirts and T-shirts.

But collectors, dealers, "pickers" (scouts for dealers), and smart buyers are at work at these auctions, too. They follow them regularly because they know there are bargains to be found, antiques or well-kept older pieces that can be bought inexpensively and resold at a profit at big-city auctions, or just taken home and enjoyed. Just as the dealers at posh auctions do their best to remain anonymous by wearing inconspicuous clothes, so the dealers or pickers at these country auctions affect the plain dress of the audience. They don't fool the auctioneers, however; at several of these country auctions, the auctioneer pointed out to me the dealers in the audience, the city slickers trying to look like their country cousins.

When a dealer bids, it's a clue that the item may be even more valuable than the auctioneer realizes, or that the dealer is trying to buy the object for a specific customer. But usefulness and need are as important as value at these auctions, including the real need for something pretty to brighten a housewife's lonely life. And these auctions also serve as the weekly social and entertainment centers; in many communities, they are the major recreation during the long winters. So, with a nod, or an open palm, or a raised index finger, bidders vie for dishes or lamps or sturdy chests from someone's farm bedroom, or old-fashioned dolls that could (if bought by a picker) end up getting fancy prices at an urban doll auction. No records are set, but the competition is keen.

In between these opposite ends of the auction spectrum is the amazingly varied middle range of auctions, continually shifting and changing so that there seems to be one that comfortably fits just about every taste and pocketbook. It's these middle "layers" that quite rightfully appeal to those of us who fit the amorphous description, "middle class." Here prices can start as low as $10 for miscellaneous cartons full of all kinds of odds and ends—silverware, brass, small pictures—typically sold quickly at the beginning to get the audience "warmed up" and to allow time for latecomers to find seats. The

average sale price can be as low as $50, though $100 may be more typical. It's at such auctions that you can indeed, as some auction houses say in their ads, furnish a room completely, *tastefully*, with quality objects, for under $5,000. I believe it's in these middle-layer auctions that the most practical buys are to be found—if you bide your time and buy carefully. And prices at these middle-level auctions often advance by $10, $20 and $25, which, speaking personally, is more to my liking than the $50, $100 and even $1,000 advances of the high-priced auctions.

Where and what are these middle-layer auctions? Here is a quick overview. They are the smaller, less well-advertised sales run by the major auction houses, sometimes in the less elegant rooms: bare floors, smaller folding chairs, plain overhead lighting fixtures. Very often,

Pre–Sale
Exhibition—
of Pickets
And Protestors

*Some auctions attract more than buyers. When Robert C. Scull, the owner of "Scull's Angels," a fleet of taxicabs in New York City, had an auction of part of his collection of modern art, there was a demonstration by a group of cabbies who were organizing a union. They picketed the auction with signs saying that Mr. Scull was "a parasite who lived off the backs of cabbies so he could be with the beautiful people." There were also demonstrations by Women in The Arts, protesting that only one woman was represented in the sale.*

*There was such a crush of people that they had to be led through the front door of Sotheby's in groups of ten. A columnist sniffed at the whole affair by writing, "The entire evening may be summed up by telling that Mrs. Scull appeared in an evening gown specially designed for the sale, decorated with the emblem of her husband's fleet of taxis."*

these are the sales that are held all year round on a specified day at a specified time, and steady buyers get to know them. If there are catalogs, they are usually black-and-white, with few, if any, pictures; or there may be just printed lists of the lots for sale.

Then there are the regular sales run by (if they will forgive me) the smaller or less prestigious auction houses, in their serviceable but plain auction rooms, with printed lists and very brief descriptions of the lots for sale.

Finally there are the on-site or estate sales, held at the homes (literally on-site) of individuals or families who are disposing of the contents of the house, yard, and garage by having an auction run by a professional auctioneer.

There are many reasons for getting good and affordable buys at these auctions. First, there's the merchandise itself. It has been culled by the auctioneer so that there is very little junk (he doesn't want to cheapen the auction) and conversely, the masterpieces have been put

aside for the special auctions. In other words, a middle range of goods, with prices to match.

Second, there's the possibility of less competition. Just because these are general rather than specialized auctions, they have a broad range of merchandise but not too much depth. When there are just a few rugs, or a few chests, or a few paintings, dealers and collectors are less likely to attend. Since their time isn't unlimited, they may decide to skip these general sales.

Third, without extensive catalogs, there is less mail order bidding, or even no mail order bids at all. Again, less competition.

Fourth, there is less publicity. The big auctions are advertised in the national media and, of course, draw a much larger audience; the smaller auctions may be advertised only in the local papers, and therefore bring only a local audience, often less knowledgeable, or less well-heeled.

*39*

Finally, and particularly at house auctions, often there are no reserves—no minimum prices set, below which the owners won't sell—because the auction is being held to settle an estate; the trustees or executors of the estate want it sold, and sold quickly, sometimes within one day only. No reserves and a necessarily fast pace often mean fast bidding and comparatively low prices.

It's at these middle-range auctions that you learn about quality and price, and realize that well-known names in the ads don't mean high prices unless the *quality* is there. I've been attracted to auctions by the names of such artists as Raphael, Soyer, and Dali, and by the promise of getting a rare bargain with a Tiffany studio vase or a signed Lalique glass bowl. But at the auctions themselves, I saw that the paintings were very small or very dull; the vase unattractive, visibly cracked and poorly repaired; the Lalique bowl quite ordinary, and the presale estimate on its value too high.

I thought that the prices some of these items "fetched," as they say in the auction world, was reasonable in the case of the Soyer—the auctioneer started the bidding at $100, got a counterbid from the floor of $60, and sold it for $80—but probably too much for the Tiffany vase, which sold for $50 with no competing bids. (The buyer, a woman, only shrugged when her husband asked, very loudly, the question in my mind and I'm sure in the mind of others: "What the hell did you buy that for?")

A word of caution here. Please note that I am speaking only in general terms: the world of auctions, including the middle world, is always full of surprises. (That's what makes auction-going such an interesting game.) There is "junk" sometimes at middle auctions, simply because everyone has his own idea as to what is and what is not junk. There are high-priced items at middle auctions ($10,000, $20,000 and up), either because they happen to be part of the merchandise that the auctioneer decides to put into that particular sale, or because some people,

## The Marriage Game at Auctions

*Goods bought at auctions can sometimes spark controversy between husband and wife, each usually questioning the judgment of the other. (Or perhaps it provides an opportunity to blow off peacefully a little marital-conflict steam.) Bruce Selkirk, of Selkirk's Galleries Auction in St. Louis, has been known to say to husbands, in his gentle voice, "Don't bid against your wife, sir. It's not good policy."*

*Sometimes, however, the controversy is simply a lighthearted expression of the indulgent-husband game. I watched one night at Sotheby's, New York, as one of their women vice-presidents bid anonymously and successfully on behalf of a customer. The painting was sold for $90,000. After the auction, I saw an elderly couple approach the vice-president. The wife gave her a hug and said, "I'm thrilled." The husband just smiled and said, "I'm bankrupt."*

for their own reasons, want something enough to bid the price way up. There are dealers and collectors at most auctions—because *they* are looking for the rare finds and the bargains.

Which brings up the next point. Who goes to these middle-level auctions? Business and professional people are one category: the top-level management executive who haunts Freeman's in Philadelphia and places absentee bids for his collection of books by French photographers and architects; the Washington businesswoman who is decorating her office with watercolors acquired at Sloan's; the midwestern college professor who collects Wedgwood during his weekend trips to auction houses near his home in Carson City, Michigan.

The fashionable are here, too—the ultra-chic couples who lend a certain pizazz to any scene. The man is often a country-gentleman type, wearing Gucci loafers and a tweed jacket with suede elbow patches. The woman may be a country-gentlewoman type, wearing her tweed

jacket and corduroy skirt, or splendid in very personal high fashion. These couples often come knowing exactly what they're looking for: cut glass, or small country chests, or antique rockers.

The remainder of the audience is completely mixed in age and type, from the long-haired young women and bearded young men in their twenties to the many greying men (balding too) and women in their sixties and seventies. Some members of the audience seem to be retirees, more interested in spending a few hours observing than in bidding. Others, particularly the middle-aged women, are often "spotters" for their married sons and daughters, who need furniture but can't come because they are on the job at home or in the office. After the successful bid, these women are likely to dash to the telephone to report that their grandchildren will soon have some "new" furniture.

42

Can you see any reason why you should be intimidated by any part of this auction scene—from the most elegant to the most ordinary? Particularly when auctioneers—also from the most elegant to the most ordinary—are continually advertising, offering more services, scheduling more exhibitions, extending their viewing hours and their auction hours because they *want* you to come. Ultimately, they want you to buy, of course, but in the beginning they are happy if you just drop in and watch, because they think once you've seen how easy it is, you're bound to become a regular customer.

But, of course, you don't want to be just a regular customer. You want to be the smart customer who understands the rules of the game and gets the best buys. To do that, you have to know more about these many layers of the auction world and about the rules—which you'll learn in the following chapters.

# 3  MEET THE AUCTIONEER

At the stage center of any auction is, of course, the auctioneer—the guru of the gavel. It's no simple job the auctioneer sets out to do. His or her main aim is to stimulate the bidding, to inveigle the audience into spending top dollar on the varied, motley items that pass the auctioneer's block. And to do this, the auctioneer must be a combination public relations man, actor, athlete, and marketing expert. Listen to the advice that auctioneers receive from the people who train them, or pass on to newcomers in the field.

"An auctioneer should have a thorough knowledge of the product he is selling, the true market value, the likes, dislikes, needs and financial capabilities of his buyers and sellers, plus good common sense."

"A successful auctioneer should be a gentleman at all times . . . play the game fairly . . . have a smile for everyone . . . a good disposition . . . be honest and not misrepresent."

"An auctioneer should learn to be a supersalesman. . . . Take every opportunity to attend other sales and hear other auctioneers even though the auctioneer might be your competitor."

"An auctioneer should have plenty of enthusiasm . . . a pleasing personality. . . . He should be witty and try to keep his audience in a jovial mood. . . . Occasionally, he should be able to tell a good joke. A short snappy joke is much better than a long one. . . . Remember that many attend auctions just to listen to the auctioneer; try to entertain them."

"An auctioneer should have plenty of vim, vigor and vitality. To make a success, you must be physically fit and mentally alert. Take care of yourself. Visit your doctor and dentist often. Breathe properly. . . . Get plenty of fresh air. . . . Get enough sleep and rest. . . . You cannot overeat, smoke too much, keep late hours and get up on the auction block and conduct a successful auction the next day. Don't dissipate."

"The good auctioneer learns how to read the crowd. He can see who is open to his enticements, who is defensive, who is thinking over the items being offered, who is rejecting the whole idea, and is suspicious, and who is ready."

The auctioneer isn't just a star, he (or she—women auctioneers are still few in number, but they're increasing) is a *superstar*. After the merchandise is acquired and the back room work is done (we'll take a peek at this behind-the-scenes stuff later in the chapter), it's the auctioneer who wheedles, coaxes, encourages—controls the bidding and brings in the dollars—and the good auctioneer never forgets it. It's part of his trade or, as he prefers to say, his profession.

*The Auctioneer's Image*

Because the auctioneer carries so much responsibility

45

for the success of the sale, important auctions are handled by the most prestigious, the most experienced, and the most knowledgeable auctioneers. When Sotheby's or Christie's, the top houses in the auction-house pecking order, have one of their super-duper, high-society, big-estate, important-collection auctions, it's John L. Marion, president and chief auctioneer at Sotheby's, or David Bathurst, president of Christie's, who wields the gavel. (There are, of course, some auction houses where the president of the company chooses not to be an auctioneer.)

And just as it's good for their respective auction houses that these two distinguished gentlemen lend their style and personal prestige to the auction block at spotlighted moments, it's also good for the image of auctioneers and the auction field as a whole—because image is important to auctioneers, something they worry

about. This image hasn't always been a good one, especially in the United States.

As we saw in Chapter One, the early colonists brought a tradition of auctions from England, where auction sales were well established and where, in 1766, James Christie founded the auction house whose American arm was so successfully established in New York in 1977. The first extensive use of auctions in the New World was for selling tobacco in Virginia. This was followed by the auctioning of great estates. Since fine household goods were not produced in great quantity in colonial America, auctions were a major source for homeowners who wanted furniture and decorations. George Washington attended such auctions, and the records show that he bid for pickle pots, pillows, and bottles, and that he bought an elegant mahogany tambour sideboard for £12 8s.

It was during the days of slavery that the reputation of

the auctioneer became tarnished. Because his main commodity was slaves and he associated with slave traders, slave keepers, and even slave kidnappers, he was not considered a very respectable citizen. This unsavory reputation was further diminished by the Civil War and its aftermath, when auctioneers followed the troops and auctioned off some of the property seized after successful battles. What's more, some colonels auctioned off the spoils of battles, which led nonarmy auctioneers doing the same thing to adopt the felt hat of the military colonels, their rank, and their frequently unscrupulous business practices.

Many auctioneers today, especially those outside the major cities, are still happy to use the title "Colonel"—but they are not so happy about the negative image of auctions and auctioneers that to a degree still exists. Many people continue to associate auctions with shoddy merchandise sold to unwitting buyers who are stimulated to bid by unidentified employees planted in the audience. So auctioneers worry about their image, are constantly working to upgrade it, and want to be known as "professionals" in the profession of auctioneering.

More and more states are now requiring some form of licensing of auctioneers. And their trade group, the National Auctioneers Association, in 1976 established an advanced training program, the Certified Auctioneers Institute, in conjunction with Indiana University at Bloomington. Applicants must have two or more years of full-time auction experience to become part of the program, which lasts for three weeks over a three-year period.

The Institute's program consists of approximately ninety hours of instruction covering management, marketing, accounting, appraisals, law, leadership, ethics, and other areas. The students must pass a three-hour exam at the end of the first week of courses to be admitted to the second level offered the next year, and then must pass the second-level exam in order to be admitted to the third level taught the *next* year. By early 1980, some 223 auctioneers had successfully completed the entire course and won the right to place CAI® (Certified Auctioneers Institute®) after their names.

*The Auctioneer Type*

Whether they've acquired their expertise from the CAI®, or from practical experience working as auctioneers—selling automobiles, businesses, government property, antiques, furniture, decorative objects, cattle, horses, jewelry, paintings, posters, photographs, farms, houses, machinery, etc., etc.—there are some characteristics auctioneers have in common. Admittedly, their speech patterns differ, from an Englishman's very correct pronunciation to a midwesterner's twang, from a southern drawl to a Brooklyn accent to a New England broad *A*. Their style on the podium also differs, from calm and quiet to a fast, fast chant. Their background varies, from farm boy to international banker, from art historian to furniture dealer. Nonetheless, all successful auctioneers share several important traits.

They are competitive—since it is a highly competitive business. They are, or learn to be, outgoing. As one of them says, "The meek will inherit the earth, but sure as hell not the auction business." Indeed, it is hard to be meek when you're on the stand, behind either a well-used pine table or a bona fide carved mahogany lectern.

Particularly if they have founded and own their auction business, auctioneers are rugged individualists who could never adjust to the confines of a nine-to-five desk job. They enjoy dealing with people, they like the excitement of the action of the auction, they have an instinct for salesmanship, they are hard-working (long hours, irregular meals), and they have "tough hides." You can't have a delicate ego, easily threatened, if you have to face audiences that are sometimes yawning, looking frankly bored, busy talking among themselves, wandering in and out, not paying any attention to you on the podium, com-

plaining loudly about your last decision to cut off bids, or showing, in one way or another, their hostility to you.

One of the best descriptions of an auctioneer comes from James Bough's book, *Auction!,* unfortunately now out of print: "Auctioneers make up a special fraternity, having more in common with each other than with their audiences whether the day's business is sculpture or a bankrupt bottling plant. . . . The accents of the art auctioneer are usually smoother, but he is the same essential mixture of croupier and hypnotist as humbler members of the brotherhood. . . ."

To which I add an "amen" and a few of my own observations. Off the block (and off the record), auctioneers have a self-deprecating sense of humor: "We are in the business of selling 300,000 things that nobody needs," says a Sotheby's vice-president. A favorite joke is about auctioning off the brains of people from various professions. "A doctor's brain goes for $500," the auctioneer will say, "a lawyer's brain for $750, but an auctioneer's brain goes for $10,000." "How come an auctioneer's brain brings such a high price?" you ask. The answer: "You don't know how many auctioneers we need to get the right brain."

Having watched a great number of auctioneers at work, I don't take this too seriously. Many have excellent academic or practical backgrounds in their specialty, whether it's paintings, antique furniture, fine jewelry, livestock, automobiles, or real estate. And what they don't know, they are eager to learn, whether from experts or from their customers. But above all, they are past masters in their understanding of human nature and how to manipulate it, though they surely wouldn't like that word *manipulate*.

### The Auctioneer's Skill

Some examples of this skill follow—remember them when you're at your next auction!

Picture this fine sixtyish southern gentleman, six feet three, very handsome with his white hair and deep blue eyes, his suntanned, almost wrinkle-free complexion, fine posture, and only the merest hint of a developing pot belly. In his wonderful deep voice, he tells how he encourages customers to bid: "You look at a customer who is interested in buying something. The opening price is $50 and you say, 'Will you give me $60?' And you shake your head slightly up and down. And the first thing you know, the person you're looking at is shaking his or her head, too, and that means, yes, they will give you $60 and then, of course, you go on to $70." Watch for that nod.

Here are the comments of another auctioneer. "Flatter your customers," he says. "You always give almost the same opening speech when you start the auction: everything's sold as is, the goods have to be removed from the premises within three days, please pay your bills at the office, et cetera. Give the speech, forget something purposely, such as the rule that no checks are accepted without proper identification. Then ask, 'Did I forget anything?' The regular customers in the audience will say, 'You forgot to say that no checks are accepted without proper identification.' They like that, they feel smart, they empathize with you for making a mistake—and part of selling is making your customers like you and identify with you and maybe feel one up on you.''

"You have to know how to arrange what's being sold to get the top bid,'' says still another auctioneer. "Say you're selling cut glass, and it's not of even quality. Separate the lots. Put the inferior stuff together in one group. People who want to bid on the inexpensive pieces can do it all at once, and since they'll be bidding against each other, they'll bid the price up. Have the superior stuff in another group, later. Then those interested in getting the better stuff will be bidding against each other—and they'll bid those prices up.''

Auctioneers get to know their customers' needs, tastes, and passions; and this applies to all levels of auctions. At an elegant estate sale, I've heard the auctioneer say in a suave voice, "This would look fine in your home, sir.'' At a middle-level sale in an urban gallery, I've heard the auctioneer tell the clerk recording the sales, "That was sold to Mr. X,'' and I've watched Mr. X's face assume the pleased look that many of us get when we're recognized as patrons. And at a country consignment auction, I've heard the auctioneer call to someone catching a smoke outside the door, "Yoo-hoo, Jody, have a look, here's a toaster coming up.'' It's all salesmanship—and it works.

As a group, I admire them, even when I find myself getting caught up in their blandishments. Some of the big-city auctioneers have an elegance about them that would make it seem natural if they kissed the hands of heiresses who had just bought million-dollar paintings—if they didn't have to continue the auction. Some west-

ern auctioneers have incredibly deep, mellow voices that are a pleasure to the ear. I can (almost) forgive the male chauvinism of many of the southerners and midwesterners, because they compliment and flatter all women equally—young, old, thin, fat, pretty, or plain. The women in the field have talent, verve, and guts, and are making good careers for themselves in what used to be men-only territory.

But, when I'm at an auction, I don't forget that in this great game for grownups, the auctioneers are the antagonists—friendly antagonists, of course—but just the same, it's my pocketbook versus their persuasive powers. So I play the game by the rules you're going to read about in the pages ahead.

But first a word about the background to an auction.

*Behind the Scenes*

Just as a star cannot turn a bad script into a smashing

success, so even a star auctioneer does not by himself make a success of the auction business—for it is a *business,* of which showmanship is just one part. If we're to be a properly appreciative audience (meaning better buyers), we should have at least a rough idea of what's happening backstage.

Where does all that stuff come from that passes under an auctioneer's gavel? With nothing to sell, there is no auction, which means the first and continuing priority of any auction house is to *get the goods.* Where? Unlike other businesses, auctioneers cannot call up a manufacturer and say, "Send me another shipment." Instead, as the French auctioneer Maurice Rheims rather grimly puts it, "Death is the supply merchant."

It's no secret that auctioneers follow the obituaries column, that they sometimes call themselves the "ghoul" department, and that, as Robert C. Woolley, a senior vice-president of Sotheby's, remarked at a world art market conference, "We look at everything in an estate except what's flat." Everything, that is, but the corpse.

Auctioneers make it their business to cultivate attorneys and bank trust officers who pick the auction house to use when they are settling an estate. (I've been told that bank officers who are trustees of an estate often know it will be coming on the block before some relatives do.) And if through the "right" background, family, or carefully cultivated social relationships, auctioneers are also known to the people who have valuable collections—so much the better. Then, when death, divorce, or a less drastic change of life makes someone decide to sell and the person wonders who will handle the transaction, the auctioneer who's familiar will come to mind. "Why not dear George? After all, he knows the family and the circumstances—and he is in the business."

Once the auction house gets the job (and the competition is getting keener every day, as the auction business expands), the real behind-the-scenes work begins. Everything must be accounted for, which could mean going through the contents of a huge estate or a small house, sometimes for weeks, and sometimes by flashlight if the power has been turned off. Every item must have a lot number, from the boxful of kitchen utensils to the difficult-to-categorize bric-a-brac that all of us accumulate, to the house furnishings, rugs, paintings, tools, yard equipment, linens, and so on, and on.

If the sale isn't being held on the premises, everything then must be moved to the auction house, a procedure that involves tedious wrapping, packing, and loading at one end, and then unloading, unwrapping, and unpacking at the other end. (If you've ever moved a household, you know what it's like. Just imagine multiplying the number of items to be moved by ten, twenty, or more, and then keeping track of them until they are put up for sale! The mind boggles, even though the auction house has a staff to do these things.)

Next comes the print work—anything from a simple

## Those Astonishing Back-room Artifacts

*The back rooms of auction houses have to be among the most fascinating hodgepodge rooms in the world. Here are some of the items I have seen in my back-room wanderings: a Spanish-style six-foot-long chest, with a worm-eaten section almost perfectly round and about as big as a dinner plate; magnificent Chinese brocade robes, hanging near African tribal masks; a sign identifying one back room as the "Chotsky Department"; a Buddha and some Indian temple carvings stored next to mounted deer heads; two ultra-modern zebra-patterned upholstered chairs next to two tiny cradles, one of them with tiny hand-painted red, black, and white flowers; a large wire screen with a pheasant and tropical birds mounted on it as if they had just alighted; two gaudy slot machines that looked as if they would certainly register "tilt" if you tried to play them; short black sequinned dresses, perfect for dancing the Charleston; magnificent sterling silver trays, of every size and degree of ornateness, in a cubicle that was literally wall-to-wall sterling objects; a greenish statue of the Hindu goddess Shiva about as tall as I am (five feet four) mounted in a wheel; paintings of pastoral scenes next to religious scenes, next to grim-faced colonial Americans; and, of course, innumerable odds and ends, all the things that we surround ourselves with for utility, comfort, aesthetic appeal, and who-knows-what human need or vanity—clocks, mirrors, desks, chairs, lamps, rugs, copying machines, TV sets, refrigerators, barbed-wire collections, butterfly collections . . .*

*To take a trip through the back rooms is to take a trip down memory lane. No matter how young or how old you are, you'll see something that reminds you of your childhood. I still cannot pass a trunk in an auction house without wondering if there's a dead body inside, as there was in the Saturday matinee movies I went to as a child. The auction staff always assures me that they've looked and there isn't.*

mimeographed list of the lot numbers to an elaborate, glossy catalog complete with photographs (some in color), carefully researched descriptions of the goods being auctioned off, and possibly even a history of previous owners, plus such information as where the art has been exhibited, measurements, and estimated sales price. All very time-consuming, requiring a staff of specialists: art historians, writers, editors, catalogers, appraisers.

Next, the setting for the "show" has to be carefully staged. Whether it's a large window fronting on a busy street, the rooms of the auction gallery, or the lawn of a private house (and not necessarily a big estate), the pieces are arranged to start your acquisitive juices flowing: a fine couch and two arm chairs of the same period may be set on a beautiful rug; perhaps sets of dishes are

57

tastefully displayed on a dining room table; boxes of odds and ends are put off in a corner so you can rummage casually and experience that there's-got-to-be-a-bargain-in-this-box feeling; glassware and small figurines are displayed in well-lit glass cases, to show their sparkle. "The furniture will be arranged much as it was when Mrs. X and her late husband returned from their frequent and regular trips abroad," to quote from one auction preview announcement. In short, salesmanship at work so that the goods look opulent, cozy, sophisticated, charming, comfortable, glamorous—whatever the particular quality that's appropriate, and *tempting*.

As you can see, before you arrive at an auction, tens if not hundreds of decisions, big and little, have been made by experts so that when you get there, you will buy! So, before you go, you should be preparing, too. And that's the general topic: how to be a savvy auction-goer. But first let's pause for one person's look at becoming an auctioneer—mine!

# 4 CALL ME COLONEL: LEARNING TO BE AN AUCTIONEER

"A school for auctioneers? I never knew they existed."
That's the usual comment I get when I show off my
fancy framed diploma from the Missouri Auction School.
The diploma "certifies" that I have "successfully completed the course of study in AUCTIONEERING,"
thereby earning not only the diploma but the right to be
called "Colonel Auerbach."

And earn it I did. For two weeks, I rarely got more than
five or six hours' sleep per night; subsisted mainly on
peaches and pumpernickel melba toast; sweated from intense heat and more intense nervousness; thanked instructors for poking me in the back with their elbows;
traveled dark country roads late at night with strangers—and loved every minute of it! They were two of the
most varied and interesting weeks of my not-so-short life.

Why did I decide to leave my nice husband, comfortable New York City apartment, and treasured swim club to travel to Kansas City, Missouri, in the heat of the summer, to learn about the auction field? Partly because, as a writer, I hoped a view from the "inside" would help me write a better book. And partly because, like everyone else, I couldn't help noticing that more and more auction houses were opening, that existing houses were expanding, and that more and more items, both old and new, were becoming collectibles sold at auction—and I was curious as to why all this was happening.

Why did I choose the Missouri Auction School, from among the fourteen or so existing schools around the country (mostly in the Midwest but also in Tennessee, Florida, and New Jersey)? Because it was the oldest (1905), because I had read that it was called the "Harvard" of auction schools, and because I was impressed that its president and owner, Richard (Dick) Dewees, had no hesitation about inviting me to come incognito, and about allowing me to write whatever I wanted to about the experience.

*The People*

Those were *my* reasons for attending. But how about my 155 classmates, 139 men and 16 women—why did they come? Money was one motivation. Some were exploring new ways to add to their current incomes by working part-time as auctioneers at about $20 an hour to $50 a day, depending on the auction. Others had heard that good full-time auctioneers could earn $40,000 to $50,000 or more per year.

Who were some of these people? There was a biscuit company salesman from California, who had been helping out at a local auction house on weekends and had already done some auctioning. His wife used her tax refund to pay for his tuition to the school. There was a Long Island Rail Road engineer, who had already started an auction business and planned to expand it when he got back to New York. There was an assistant principal from Flint, Michigan, who had been the volunteer auctioneer at fund-raising auctions for his school. He planned to earn money weekends and summers working as an auctioneer.

There were several schoolteachers from the West looking for alternatives to teaching, in view of declining enrollments. And two Mid-South school system administrators, who had plans for running an antique and auction business during the summers. There was a high school teacher from Georgia, who already ran an antiques business part-time, and a college professor from Michigan, who ran a small mail-order business and dabbled in antiques. Both of them planned to add auctioneering to their antique business. Both had driven to school in their vans, and were busy buying items at the nightly auctions in the area to take back and sell.

Some were at the school because auctioneering was part of their work already, and they wanted to either know more about it or be able to take over the business themselves. Two women antique dealers, one from New Hampshire and one from Oregon, intended to expand into antique auctions as supplements to their thriving businesses. A former furniture store owner from Colorado, whose business had been hard hit by the recession, had converted his store into a successful auction house and proudly said he had one of the most attractive auction houses in the West, since the space had been a furniture showroom. He'd been paying an auctioneer, and decided he wanted to do the auctioning himself. His teenage daughter was enrolled with him, so she could help out while pursuing her acting and singing career. (They were both good auctioneers, with good voices—but she was better.)

There was a former Minnesota farmer who worked for a company that held weekly auctions of new furniture: manufacturers overstock, odd pieces, slightly damaged

## Indoor Sport: Sniping at The Auction

*If you're unhappy that your estate won't be written up in the paper when it's auctioned off, console yourself with the thought that some reporters and newspaper people might have chosen the occasion to write snide things about you.*

*Take the comments on the estate auction of Kathryn Miller, also known as Kitty Miller, the daughter of Jules Bache, the investment banker. She had married Gilbert Miller, the Broadway producer, and they were known for their wealth and their style of living. She had a fifteen-room Park Avenue apartment, a Connecticut farm, a London house, a fourteenth-century estate in Sussex, England, a Paris apartment, a villa in Biarritz, France, a mansion on the island of Majorca, and a country house on Long Island, New York. The newspaper stories about the auction said that, in these many homes, for nearly sixty years she pursued with "staggering zeal" her desire to be known as an international hostess.*

*Mr. Miller was described in one story as a fat, gross-looking man with slits for eyes, and a double chin that covered his entire throat. His renown as a producer was almost equaled by his reputation for snobbery, said one writer; he "really prefers the company of Duchesses."*

*Mrs. Miller, the press said, always made the best-dressed list—but never at the top. When her clothes were auctioned, they drew "considerably less-heated bidding, probably because of her Amazonian size sixteen." Another writer said she was "noted more for her lifestyle than her taste in art."*

*Christie's was the auction house running the Miller sale, and they gave a party just before the auction. Some two hundred of her "friends" were invited to Christie's East to celebrate the mementos of her life. "It was a motley group," said the newspapers. One woman guest wore a Davy Crockett hat; another had on purple slacks with a striped beige mink jacket. Only one man came in black tie and dinner jacket, but there were*

*many in slacks and sports shirts. Everyone was drink-*
*ing, laughing, chatting, and only occasionally looking*
*at the household treasures Kathryn Miller had taken a*
*lifetime to collect.*

goods. He already knew quite a bit about his company, but wanted to learn how to auction. His counterpart from New York was a government employee who worked for a General Services Administration office that sold excess government equipment, sometimes through auctions— and he wanted to be the auctioneer. (The government was paying his way, and as a taxpayer, you'll be glad to know that he really watched every penny, kept a meticulous record of his expenses.) And there was a five-foot, ninety-some-pound, pipe-smoking woman owner of a used-furniture store who planned to expand her business into auctions.

The real-estate industry formed a special group, since only salespeople who had licenses or were in the process of acquiring them were admitted to the special real-estate seminars, while the rest of us were busy in other classes practicing our chants or learning how to open an auction. Some of the real-estate people were successful brokers, some aspired to be. But all believed—and this is the interesting point—that the coming thing would be more auctions of private houses and condominiums. Their seminars were usually taught by Bill Morgan, a former small-town bank president who decided to become an auctioneer when he found that "the checks he cashed for auctioneers were larger than his salary as a bank president."

The good old American entrepreneurial spirit pervaded the school. Again and again, people told me they wanted to go into business for themselves, they thought auctioneering was one way to do it, and they were more than willing to put in the long hours and hard work (and that's the score for auctioneers) in order to be indepen-

dent. Most of them had been affected by changes in the economy. For instance, a former civil engineer from Pennsylvania had worked for a coal broker and had loved flying around in the company plane, but found the coal market so erratic that he decided he had to go into some other business. Several men had worked for a marine company in the Pacific Northwest. It was their opinion, and they were bitter about it, that because of U.S. government regulations, they had been forced out of the tuna fishing business. They had been replaced by Japanese companies, who weren't subject to the same restrictions. Since one of them had had to sell his tuna boat, they understood only too well that there were good opportunities at boat auctions.

There was a snowmobile dealer who realized that the

uncertain supply and high price of gasoline made his business precarious; a former car dealer, who sold his dealership just before the collapse of the auto market; a plant wholesaler who was going into plant auctions (who organized the first student beer-and-pizza party); and an advertising man and his stunning girl friend (how the young men in the class sighed when she got up to auction), who were interested in auctioneers as clients.

Not surprisingly, since the school's sessions are held (four times a year) in the Missouri Livestock Exchange Building, in America's heartland, there was also a fairly large contingent of young farmers. Many of them had grown up going to farm and livestock auctions, and they were "naturals" when it came to mastering the auctioneers' chants. Like me, though, they had an image problem. In my case, I was forever defending New York City, and assuring people that I really could walk on the streets at night, that I had seen trees before, that I had never been mugged, that I knew my next-door neighbor, and that not all New Yorkers were mean. In their case, they were inclined to be quiet during conversations at lunch, because they assumed everyone thought they were "hicks" who could talk only about cows and chickens.

One of the star chanters among the group was Junior from Arkansas. But, in contrast to those of us who had to learn to speed up, Junior had to learn to slow down. We would sit and listen to his racing chant, fascinated, but not able to follow his bids. The instructors urged him to practice slowing down after the regular class sessions.

Like many of us, Junior was nervous, and he developed a habit of practicing in his sleep! (I'm not joking.) This didn't affect his roommate (most students doubled), who fortunately was a sound sleeper. Unfortunately, another classmate, Jim, had a room across the court and *was* a light sleeper. One night, so Jim told us, he woke up about 2:00 a.m., heard Junior chanting and couldn't get back to sleep. Finally he yelled, "Sell it!" In his sleep, Junior said, "Sold to the lady in the first row," and shut up. (That's Jim's story anyway.)

These young men were the style setters for the class in their big white "good guy" felt or straw hats, decorated with fancy feather bands; their tooled leather, high-heeled cowboy boots, and their fancy leather belts with silver buckles. Their hats were so dear to them, as they were to some of the auctioneer-instructors, that the only time they took them off—and then with loud groans of protest—was for the class graduation picture, when they were forced to so they wouldn't obscure the faces of the people sitting behind them. Before the end of the two-week session, at least another third of the class had weakened and bought similar hats. (Admittedly, the hats are useful when conducting an outdoor auction, as a sunshade and to help the audience keep its eye on you. But indoors? All day? No way.)

Where did the people come from geographically? There were few states that weren't represented, and there were even two Canadians, one from Ontario and one from Quebec. Not surprisingly, there was a large contingent from Missouri, since the school was in Missouri; but there was also a large group from Michigan, again not surprisingly, since Michigan was so hard hit by the recession in the automobile industry that many people were being forced to look for new careers.

With such a variety of geographical origins, there was also a tremendous variety of accents, and it led to one of the nicest features of the school, the meeting of East and West, North and South, different worlds. Some were amused by my eastern accent; I was intrigued by the southern and western accents, though there were times when I, and others, found them difficult to understand.

There was also a great range of ages, from teenagers with their parents to seventy-year-olds. The youngest person on his own was Chris from Kansas. He was sixteen; he had earned part of his tuition and his family had given him the remainder. He had one of the fanciest

hats, and the loudest whistle when a pretty girl got up to auction. He had just received his driver's license, and his father said he could drive to school—until he got his first ticket. "So," Chris told us, "I'm the safest driver in Kansas City and on the Missouri highways."

*A Day in the Auction School*

The school doesn't operate full-time, but has four two-week sessions during the year. In between, all the instructors are otherwise occupied: running their own auction businesses; selling all kinds of real estate (ranches, farms, private houses); selling estates; judging cattle; taking an active part as elected officers of the National Auctioneers Association; and competing in national contests for the best auctioneer's chant, judged not only for speed, endurance, and mellowness, but also for clarity. As a group, they are hardworking, competitive, aggressive, keen-minded businessmen who enjoy their work. They are secure enough financially and personally to take a real interest in the students, and to expect them to do their best, which meant working hard for the two weeks. And work hard we did. For the rest of this chapter, I'm going to describe a typical day at the school, to show you how hard.

*7:00:* The desk clerk at the motel calls and wakes me. I wash, dress, have an orange and melba toast, head down to the restaurant in the motel to pick up a cup of coffee to go, and sit with some of my classmates in the motel lobby, waiting for the yellow school bus to pick us up at 7:50 and take us to the school.

On the bus, some people are studying their books, some are practicing their chants, but most of us sit and talk. This day, the conversation turns to the long hours that auctioneers work: before a big sale, it can be twelve hours a day, seven days a week, for several weeks. And the fact that "death is the supply merchant."

The conversation shifts. Ken says his boss takes something like twelve different vitamins a day, C, D, E, and a calcium supplement. We ask how old he is, and are surprised to hear he's only forty-one. Jim says he doubts the vitamins will do him any good, and that if he dies young, don't say we didn't warn him. Someone says, "Well, if he dies on the block, you could just auction him off. You could say, 'Everything is sold as is. This body is in fine condition—everything works except the heart.' " We laugh a bit sheepishly.

*8:25:* We arrive at the school, the top floor of the weather-beaten solid old Livestock Exchange Building right across from the stockyards in Kansas City, Missouri. We head for the large meeting room where we assemble every morning. As usual, some of the class are already busy auctioning. Some do it just for practice—"selling" the school's chairs and tables. But others

68

sell what they bought at the auctions where they worked (as student auctioneers) the night before. Lynne is not having much luck selling an antique lamp until Sandy, the antique dealer from Oregon, gets up and tells the class she could get $50 for it back home. It sells for $20. Then someone auctions very attractive small wire sculptures, including figures of auctioneers, that he's brought along from home. They sell out fast, and he promises to bring more tomorrow.

*9:00:* Boyd Michaels, the school registrar, comes in and class starts on the dot, as usual. He calls the roll—no absentees, which is fairly typical. On the first day, he stated flatly that there were *no excuses* for being absent or late, including drinking too much the night before or oversleeping. The few latecomers usually have had problems with their cars; the class is serious.

*9:00–9:50:* Morning lecture. This morning, it's on the importance of appearance, manner, and manners. Question from the floor: "Is it okay to chew tobacco, if you can do it inconspicuously?" Answer: "You should not chew tobacco, because when you chew, you have to spit; and when you spit, you're liable to spit on the boots of somebody who could be a good customer. He'll never forgive you, he'll never buy from you, and he'll never give you an assignment as an auctioneer."

Reminder from the instructor: If you're going to start your own auction business and you'll be accepting consignments, don't call your place an auction "barn" or you'll get barn stuff. Call it an "auction center."

*10:00–10:50:* Our daily number and chanting practice drills, to teach us breath control and how to be comfortable when chanting number bids quickly. In the beginning, we simply stood and chanted, faster and faster, "ten, twenty, thirty, forty," and so on; then back down, "forty, thirty, twenty, ten." But now we're encouraged to add hand gestures and "bodytalk," turning first to the buyer on the right, then the one on the left, saying, "It's yours for $100, $110," and on up.

69

## Mixed Motives at Court–Ordered Auction

*Not all auctions are social events, and not all the people who go to them want to be identified.* The Wall Street Journal, *not the family or amusement pages of* The New York Times, *reported on the court-ordered auction of the estate of Sam Giancana. Mr. Giancana had built up his estate from an enterprise that included gambling, loansharking, prostitution, labor-racketeering, and extortion. At one time, the enterprise brought in $2 billion a year. His share of the "take" was about $50 million. Mr. Giancana was head of the Chicago syndicate—but he died without a will. The court ordered the sale to pay off the estate's debts and to provide for his three grown daughters.*

*The court records showed a modest estate worth only about $130,000. But it included, to the surprise of outsiders, antique porcelain figurines, delicate gold music boxes, fine Meissen dinnerware, copies of two Frank Sinatra films* (The Man with the Golden Arm *and* The Manchurian Candidate)*—as well as a film entitled* Always In My Heart, *a sentimental story about a convict who goes to prison and, when he returns, tries to win back the love of his daughter.*

*About 250 people came to the auction, including Mr. Giancana's three daughters and many antique dealers. One of them said Mr. Giancana bought his fine art from dealers and had a reputation for honesty and never reneging. (This didn't extend to his criminal activities, apparently, since he was done in by the mob after accepting a grand-jury grant of immunity.) The audience also included former neighbors, artists, collectors, and the just plain curious. Most of the buyers were dealers, however, and they hesitated to identify themselves. One of them probably expressed the view of the others when he said, "Just say that I thought it would be interesting to own something that belonged to a notorious gangster."*

In the middle of one of these exercises, with 156 people standing around gesturing and chanting, I stop and
survey the room. I get the feeling that a spectator from
another planet would look at us and report back that we
were some strange tribe, practicing a new kind of religious ritual to unknown gods on our right and our left.

*11:00–11:50:* We break into small groups with individual instructors, who will call on us to practice auctioneering; our classmates serve as the audience. Though I
have had extensive experience teaching at a university
and speaking to groups of several hundred persons
around the United States, I am so nervous that I sit in
the back of the room so I'll be one of the last to be called
on. We are warned not to say "I *got* twenty," because *got*
not only sounds harsh but is also very hard on the throat.
The instructor stands nearby and when I forget and say
"I got," he gives me a very gentle nudge in the back with
his elbow. It's an effective reminder. All the instructors
are helpful and supportive; everyone is criticized but not
demeaned.

It takes me a while to learn the chant, since I am more
accustomed to the talking method of auctioneering, but I
get it after enough mass practice sessions, and with the
encouragement of my classmates in the small groups.
We form a close bond as we struggle together to be comfortable in front of the group, to catch all the bids, to be
able to jump the bids by $2.50 or $5 or $20, without get-
ting rattled. Boyd Michael, the instructor, tells us that
the first time he got up to auction, he was so nervous that
his mouth popped open, his eyes clamped shut, and he
thought he would never get started.

*1:00:* We stop for lunch, and several of us pick up a
sandwich from the first-floor cafeteria, or fresh fruit from
a street vendor, and head for our favorite lunch spot: the
livestock auction held in the building next door. During
the ten-minute breaks between the morning sessions,
we've watched through the windows as real cowboys
herd a shipment of cattle into the pens in the stockyards

next to the Livestock Exchange Building. Now we take our seats in the visitors section and watch as the cattle are walked through the ring, while the auctioneer rattles off numbers so fast we can't understand any of it.

It doesn't matter, because the dealers, sitting in their own section, wearing their cowboy hats, do understand. They use their hand calculators and the phones hooked up right at their seats to call cattle brokers in Chicago and tell them what prices the cattle are getting.

2:00–2:50: More lectures and more practice drills. This time, we concentrate on better enunciation by practicing, faster and faster, some tongue twisters: "Rubber baby buggy bumper" or "Tommy Atata took two T's and tied them to the top of two tall trees" or "Round the rough and rugged rock the ragged rascal ran."

3:00–3:50: Another lecture, this time on getting started as auctioneers. The instructor repeats what others have mentioned: A responsible auctioneer does not take advantage of the elderly. (I heard this warning so often that I began to think the possibility was a more common occurrence than auctioneers were willing to admit.) Student question: "Couldn't I offer to run some auctions for the elderly for a lower commission, or even no commission, just to get started?" Answer: "No. The elderly wouldn't believe you." Consensus in after-class discussion: sad but true. The people would be too suspicious of the auctioneer's motives.

*4:00–5:00:* In small groups, we practice giving an opening speech with which to start an auction. We have to cover ten points: Call the crowd together to start, welcome the audience, introduce yourself, give the reason for the sale, praise the owner, introduce him, give the order of the sale (for example, "We'll start with the paintings and then go on to the silver"), give the terms and conditions of the sale, introduce the sales force, and ask for questions. (Check out the auctioneer at the next auction you attend and see if he covers these points.)

Like most of the other students, I have written an outline of my talk and practiced it the night before. I've invented a divorced couple, known for their fine taste in antiques, who are selling the contents of their Park Avenue apartment in New York because they are each moving to different parts of the country. I have great fun introducing Mr. X on one side of the room and Mrs. X on the other, but I'm still more nervous than I've ever been facing a new class, an auditorium of strangers, or even an interview on a TV or radio show. In fact, when the instructor signals that I can sit down, I drop into my chair and notice that my heart is beating so fast I can actually see my pulse palpitating. (I've since been told by some auctioneers that it's taken them from several months up to two years to be comfortable in front of an audience.)

*5:00:* The yellow school bus is waiting to take us back to our motels. But tonight (and some other nights as well), I don't head back to the motel but share a ride with two classmates, Judy and Sally. We are to take turns auctioneering at Stukes Auction, more than an hour's

73

drive away in Topeka, Kansas. The auction starts at 7:00; we want to get there before it starts, so we plan to stop for gas but not for dinner. Fortunately, though, it's June, the weather is mild and lovely, and to me the Kansas countryside, slightly rolling and very green, looks beautiful. We stop at a supermarket near Stukes Auction, buy lettuce, peaches, peanuts, and bananas, and sit on a low stone ledge outside the market, munching on these goodies. We have forgotten to buy gas.

Stukes is run by Susan Stukes, twenty-six, slim, pretty, with a creamy complexion, dark curly hair, blue eyes, and an inexhaustible supply of energy. She had been an accounting major at Washburn College in Topeka, but after three years decided she wanted to be in business, so she left and opened Stukes Auction House, which she runs with the help of her father, who does a bit of everything, and her mother, who works as cashier. She is a graduate of the auction school, and is its only woman instructor.

Once a month, Stukes has relatively formal auctions, with antiques or new merchandise, but tonight—like every Wednesday—is consignment night. People have been depositing all kinds of things on the loading platform all day, and the auction's about to begin.

The audience is made up of local farmers and millhands with their respective spouses, and other local people, most of them in overalls, or cotton blouses and skirts, or jeans. Many come every Wednesday evening whether or not they intend to bid (and many do not), just to have something to do. Boxes are unpacked right on a long table, and if there's no interest in a set of kitchen canisters, for instance, Mr. Stukes or Susan will start "pyramiding," adding items to the lot to make it more enticing. There is much whooping and hollering as a set of tools is added, or a flowerpot, or a candleholder, until the bidding finally starts. When a small bicycle appears, Mr. Stukes, about six feet tall and lean, rides it up and down the front row to show it's in good condition.

One of the neighbors comes in with a baby skunk that's been "sanitized," and carries it around so the children and many grown-ups can pet him. There's a crib on sale, and one of the customers' babies is put in it where he plays happily while the auction goes on. Every hour, Susan calls out a number and the winner gets a free Coke, to some applause.

My classmates and I are lined up waiting our turns to go on, while the ring men keep pulling things out of a box or lining up items on the long table just below the platform. It's a cement block building, without air-conditioning, and we're all sweating. Too soon, my turn comes, and I sit on the stool while Susan reassures me and whispers into my ear the price at which I should

start the bidding. (As we'll see, that's one of the trickier parts of running a successful auction.)

Just about the first thing pulled out of the box is a size 32A lilac-colored, much-washed bra, which I offer to the crowd as a fine "unmentionable," because somehow or other I can't get myself to use the word bra in that family-type audience. Next, I sell three wooden fenceposts, useful on a farm; a small refrigerator; a box of firecrackers; and a fine wooden rolling pin, which has a date carved in it that I'm too nervous to read properly. When I step down, the audience applauds for me, as they kind-heartedly do for all the students.

Then I go and join my classmates in the audience, and like them, I can't resist buying something myself. I have my heart set on a little blue robot with silver eyes and, on

76

his chest, a TV screen that flashes moon landing pictures. He walks when you turn a little handle. I win the bid for him at $4.50, and Bill, a classmate sitting next to me, suggests that I call him "Topeka." (Topeka gets a place of honor guarding our TV set when I get him back to New York.)

We head back to our motel about 11:00 and have some anxious moments looking for a place to buy the gas we forgot to buy earlier. At one point, Judy mentions that two men in a pickup truck are following us. Each of us makes a mental note of this but says nothing, quietly thinking what we will do if they continue to follow us and get unpleasant when we stop for gas. Finally, with a tank that registers empty, we find an open station. The men jump out of their truck. We brace ourselves. One of them says, "Aren't you from the Missouri Auction School?" We nod yes. He says, "So are we. We're lost and because we saw your Kansas City license, we took it for granted you would know your way back to the motel and that's why we've been following you."

We get back to the motel about 12:30, and the last thing I do before I collapse into bed is call the desk and ask them to wake me at 7:00 as usual.

# PART TWO

# PLAYING TO WIN

# 5  KNOW BEFORE YOU GO: THE SMART MIND-SET

There's a saying in the real-estate field that three things are important when it comes to buying property: location, location, and location. And there are three things you need for pleasant and successful auction-going: knowledge, knowledge, and knowledge. Ideally, gaining knowledge should start before you ever set foot in an auction gallery, and it won't stop even when you have set foot back in your own home, with your auction bargain ready to be hung, set in place, or added to your collection.

*Gearing Up*

The kind of knowledge you need depends partly on what you are looking for at an auction. Are you looking for rugs to use as wall decorations or rugs to use on your floors? Do you want a fine antique chest to add to the decor of your dining room, or several good sturdy chests to be used in your children's rooms? Are you interested in acquiring some art to enhance your home? Are you planning to start a collection—of anything from colored glass bottles to zodiac signs? All these wants can be filled at auctions, at good prices, by the sensible auction-goer who learns the rules of the game. And one primary rule of the game is: Do your homework.

The particular form your homework takes obviously depends on your interests. If you are going to auctions to acquire any kind of decorative object, antique, or collectible, you need some background. With the time and the inclination, you may become an expert. But in the beginning, you should consult the work of the existing experts to learn what has been done and what is still being done in your field of interest. (You'll enjoy this, I assure you.)

You have at your disposal various "free" universities: libraries, where you may be amazed at the material available; museums, with their permanent collections and changing exhibitions; and specialized magazines and newsletters (every field, no matter how mundane, exotic, or esoteric, seems to have its own newsletter). Plus those ever-changing "schools," the antique shows, antique shops, and flea markets—and, of course, the auctions themselves. (Auction ads usually appear in your local newspapers in the Friday, Saturday and/or Sunday editions.) The more you read and observe, the more knowledgeable you become.

Finally, depending on the extent of your interest, you may want to take courses in your special field. Here too you will find many opportunities, for not only universities, but also museums and, increasingly, auction houses themselves are offering courses in all aspects of art history, antiques, collecting, furniture restoration, and so on.

This is exactly how dealers learn their trade, so they can buy intelligently at auctions and—after adding a

sum to cover their expenses, salaries, and a profit—sell to you. They study art and furniture history, go to museums, trade shows, shop at each other's shops, and go to auctions for auctioneers and dealers only, as well as auctions open to the public. They usually become specialists in a particular field, or several fields, have a working knowledge of others, and in general draw on the knowledge of friends and competitors, collectors, and specialists in the auction houses, so that they buy at the "right" price—which for them is a price low enough to yield a profit when they resell.

Suppose you want to buy objects for your home, not necessarily antiques? The key is *comparison*. What have similar articles sold for recently? What does such and such an item usually sell for when it's new, when it's been copied, or when it's been used? Unless you have a standard of comparison, whether you are talking about sets of dishes, imported rugs, posters, tools, furniture, or machinery, you won't know if you are getting a good buy or if—it's possible—you're being ripped off.

You learn these comparative values by attending auctions, investigating the prices at dealer's shops, and reading the magazines and newsletters that report regularly on actual prices as well as price trends. For the virtues of comparison shopping, consider the experience of my dentist, a weekend farmer. (He abhors the description "gentleman farmer" which he says doesn't do justice to the hard farm work he does, but he doesn't mind being called a "gentleman dentist," because of his fine light touch with his dentist's drill). Dr. Shelby is a veteran auction-goer, so when he needed a hay rake to hitch to his tractor on his farm in upstate New York, he went to the local auction. He saw three slightly used hay rakes, any one of which would have been suitable. But the presale estimates of about $900 were, to use his word, "obscene." (A presale estimate is almost self-explanatory: the auctioneer's guess—and hope!—about the price that an object will sell for at the auction.)

On the way home he stopped at a dealer's shop in Massachusetts and saw a reconditioned hay rake, just the kind he had been looking for. "How much?" asked Dr. Shelby. "Well," said the dealer slowly, "it is used; $500 plus $100 for delivery." "Sold," said Dr. Shelby. (When the dealer discovered that his farm wasn't too far away, he charged only $25 for delivery.)

Why were the gentleman farmers at the original auction willing to pay so much more than an average dealer might charge? Because, according to Dr. Shelby, they all know each other and like to demonstrate their casual approach to money. Their attitude is, "I can afford it. So what if it's another thousand dollars?" Since Dr. Shelby is not that much of a gentleman farmer, he wisely stayed out of the bidding and ultimately got a much better buy.

*Cataloging the Sales*

At this point in your self-education (whatever your interest), you've certainly noticed that some auctions have a catalog and some do not; that some catalogs are quite fancy, with their beautiful color pictures, while some are quite plain, with maybe a few black-and-white illustrations; and that many auctions forego catalogs altogether and simply have lists of the lots for sale.

In some ways the differences in the catalogs reflect the different layers of the auction world that we discussed earlier. In general, auction houses publish more elaborate catalogs for their special sales of expensive and unusual objects or prestigious collections, and much simpler catalogs for their regular biweekly or monthly sales. So the presence and the character of the catalog tends to reflect the level of the sale it describes.

For example, one sale at an auction house will feature fine English and French furniture; another sale at the same house will feature not-so-fine furniture, which may include some English and French pieces. The first sale will probably be publicized with a fairly elaborate catalog, showing, in a mix of both color and black-and-white photographs, some of the most important pieces. The second sale will probably have only a plain black-and-white catalog or perhaps simply a list of lot numbers.

But this doesn't mean that there are not good buys at sales with fancy catalogs, nor, conversely, that you won't find high prices at some sales that have not-so-fancy catalogs. It simply indicates a difference in the rarity, artistry and background of the items being offered. (And no one can ever foretell what the final prices will be at any auction; the moment of truth comes only at the final stroke of the auctioneer's hammer.)

Catalogs are good reference books for any auction-goer, and I think you'll find it worthwhile to invest in at least one from a major auction house that you might patronize, either in person or by mail. The catalogs are usually available several weeks before a sale, giving you time not only to examine the catalog and plan to bid, but

also, if presale estimates are included, to do some comparison shopping.

In addition, the money you spend on catalogs can be a good investment, not just for an individual sale but also for the general information in them. The individual catalogs range in price from about $5 to $12, including postage. (Occasionally they may cost as much as $20 to $25 for very unusual sales, when the catalogs include many full-color illustrations and may be hardbound.)

What kind of information makes it worthwhile to buy at least one catalog and hold onto it? Here's a list; it's not all-inclusive, but does cover the major points.

• The house terms for buying and selling, including fees, commissions, when you must remove your property, what's acceptable as payment (cash, checks, possibly credit cards), services offered (absentee bids, after-sale prices).

85

- Explanation of the terms used in the catalog.
- The guarantees and warranties the house offers (you'll discover that these are minimal).
- A glossary of terms used in the catalog descriptions (more of this later).

In addition to these general statements, which give you a "feel" for the auction world as well as a record of how that particular auction house conducts its business, catalogs will very often include all or some of the following information, depending on what is being put on the block:

- For works of art, the artist or sculptor, the object's provenance (previous owner or owners), museums where it has been exhibited, books or catalogs in which it has been described—all of which contribute to authenticity.
- Presale estimates (which we'll talk about in the next chapter).
- Sometimes an asterisk or other symbol indicating

## Attribution: The Key Is in the Wording!

*One standard catalog describes the attribution of paintings, pictures, drawings, prints, and miniatures in these terms. I've given an imaginary artist the name of Silvio Juan Doe.*

| | |
|---|---|
| 1. *Silvio Juan Doe* | *In our opinion a work by the artist.* |
| 2. *Attributed to Silvio Juan Doe* | *In our qualified opinion a work of the period of the artist which may be in whole or part the work of the artist.* |
| 3. *Circle of Silvio Juan Doe* | *In our qualified opinion a work of the period of the artist and closely related to his style.* |
| 4. *Studio of; Workshop of Silvio Juan Doe* | *In our qualified opinion a work possibly executed under the supervision of the artist.* |
| 5. *School of Silvio Juan Doe* | *In our qualified opinion by a pupil or follower of the artist.* |
| 6. *Manner of Silvio Juan Doe* | *In our qualified opinion a work in the style of the artist, possibly of a later period.* |
| 7. *After Silvio Juan Doe* | *In our qualified opinion a copy of the work of the artist.* |
| 8. *Signed* | *Has a signature which in our qualified opinion is the signature of the artist.* |
| 9. *Bears signature* | *Has a signature which in our opinion might be the signature of the artist.* |
| 10. *Dated* | *Is so dated and in our qualified opinion was executed at about that date.* |
| 11. *Bears Date* | *Is so dated and in our qualified opinion may have been executed at about that date.* |

that a particular item has a reserve price on it, which means that it will be withdrawn if no one offers the minimum price set by the owner. More about this below.

• Sometimes very interesting biographical supplements about an artist, or historical background on an unusual offering.

• Information on the style, patterns, colors of various objects; the number of ounces of sterling silver in a particular piece; measurements of furniture.

• Description of major defects or restoration. Note the word *major;* minor defects are usually not described.

Some of the major houses, Christie's and Sotheby's for example, offer annual subscriptions to all their catalogs in a particular field: such as all old-master paintings sales, or contemporary prints sales, or fine jewelry sales. If you are interested in becoming a collector, you may want to subscribe, which can cost anywhere from about $20 to $100 or more, depending on the number of sales per year. (Sotheby's, which has so often been the pacesetter in services offered by auction houses, includes in the price of any of its catalog subscriptions postsale results and its monthly *Newsletter,* which reports on upcoming auctions at its salesrooms worldwide. Christie's also offers its newsletter, *News from Christie's,* free to catalog subscribers.)

About reserves: In theory, all pieces go on the auction block to be sold at whatever price competition bidding will bring. In practice, it doesn't always work that way. Not all auction houses permit reserves, but when they do, the owner of an object can set a minimum price, or reserve, and refuse to sell it unless the bidding reaches that price. (In some parts of the country a reserve is called a "protect.") If the object doesn't meet its reserve, it's "bought in," that is, the auctioneer takes it back and it may revert to the owner or be reconsigned later, depending on the particular owner or the auction house. Sometimes a catalog will have a symbol that indicates that certain items have a reserve—perhaps an asterisk.

## Furniture Labels: More Careful Wording

*The origin of furniture raises many questions. Here is another mini-glossary from a second catalog that explains some typical headings, in this case for English furniture.*

*1. GEORGE III MAHOGANY CHEST OF DRAWERS, Third Quarter 18th Century—*
*This heading, with date included, means that the piece is, in our opinion, of the period indicated with no major alteration or restoration.*

*2. GEORGE III MAHOGANY CHEST OF DRAWERS—*
*This heading, without inclusion of the date, indicates that in our opinion, the piece, while basically of the period, has undergone significant restoration or alteration.*

*3. GEORGE III STYLE MAHOGANY CHEST OF DRAWERS—*
*The inclusion of the word "STYLE" in the heading indicates that in our opinion the piece was made as an intentional reproduction of an earlier style.*

(Sometimes the fact that there are reserves is simply not mentioned at all, either in the catalog or at the auction. The auctioneer is not obligated to announce this information.)

Whatever the type of catalog, it will inevitably point up the special feature of the auction market: that everything is sold *as is.* Whether you read this in a catalog, on a list of lots, or hear the auctioneer say it before he starts a sale—and customarily the warning is both written and then repeated verbally—*take the warning literally.* You'll note in the fine print of any auction catalog that guarantees are minimal and the only claim you might have against an auctioneer is that his catalog description was not substantially correct, as measured by an impartial interpretation of that description. *As is* really means *as is.*

Auction houses assume that their customers come to

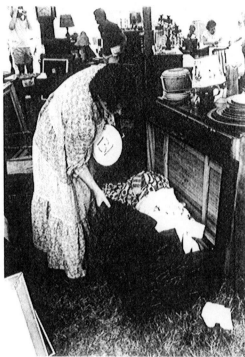

the exhibition and see the condition of the things they buy. If customers are bidding by mail order, they should assume that furniture that's been used will have some defects. Here is how one auction catalog stated their disclaimer; the warning could apply to many sales (despite the fact that catalogs sometimes do mention major defects): "No mention of age cracks, scratches, chips or other minor damages, imperfections or restorations will be made in the individual catalog entries."

### Checking Out the Goods

Catalogs are one way of finding out about the merchandise being sold at an auction. There is a better way: going to see it at the exhibitions held before the sale,

sometimes several days before, sometimes only for an hour or two on the day of the sale.

How important are the exhibitions to you as a potential buyer? To quote one of New York .City's major antique dealers: "Only a fool goes in and bids without going to the exhibition and examining everything carefully." This pronouncement is absolutely standard advice, offered by all auctioneers and veteran auction-goers, and yet, to my surprise, I found that many people just don't go to the presale exhibitions.

*Why* should you go? Because it's at the exhibitions that you duplicate the experience of the people who actually work at the auction houses and who acquire their expertise as they catalog, tag, and in other ways handle the goods that are going to be auctioned off. There is no better way, the auction people say, to learn both to appreciate quality and to spot defects.

The exhibitions give you the chance, in an unhurried atmosphere, to examine whatever you are interested in buying. And examine it you should: Open every drawer, look at front and back, run your fingers over the rims of plates, try the handles, see if the lamps light, count the saucers. (A little later I'll list some tools of the trade that will make this job easier.)

On occasion, some items are so delicate or so precious that you will hesitate to touch them. In that case, there are usually employees of the auction house who will unlock the china closet for you, or hold up a piece for viewing, or plug in a lamp if it's supposed to be in working order. (There are also people on hand who can give you some idea, if there is no catalog with presale estimates, as to what something may sell for. If they are knowledgeable, you can learn a great deal from them.)

Another reason for going to the exhibitions is to examine the box lots. These are, quite literally, boxes in which the auctioneer has combined similar items that probably wouldn't sell individually but make a tempting surprise package when put together. (On the basis of such lots, many auctioneers would qualify as Ph.D.s in psychology, with no training except their shrewd observations on how people react.) Scrounging through the boxes can be a fascinating and sometimes worthwhile occupation, as long as you're careful not to get carried away and hook yourself on buying things you'll never use.

Here's a tip of the trade: As you go through the boxes you may see something you believe has real value. Make a note to yourself to bid on that box lot. Then, if you are the successful bidder, you can take out the piece that is valuable and reconsign the remainder to be sold at another auction—sometimes even later in the same auction, if it's a small auction being run informally.

Dr. Lee Schreiber, now a professor of art history, re-

## Cracking The Auctioneer's Code

*Sometimes items are marked with the special auctioneer's code. One code word is "blacksmith." Notice that it is a ten-letter word and each letter is different. Auctioneers assign a different number, from one through ten, to each letter. B–L–A–C–K–S–M–I–T–H is the equivalent of 1–2–3–4–5–6–7–8–9–0. So if you see an item that is marked B–K–H, that would mean the house estimates the price to be $150—B being 1, K being 5, and H being 0. Another code word, or in this case words, is "gold buys it," which again is a series of ten letters, each different. Then the ticket might say G–T–T, which would be an estimate of $100.*

members his days as a dealer/wholesaler to other antique dealers. He always made it a practice to examine the box lots. At one auction he noticed a box lot of rolled-up mats and related items such as shawls and small rugs, among them a small Oriental silk rug. He bought the lot for $12.50, took out the silk rug and reconsigned the lot, which later sold for $22.50, putting him ahead of the deal. He next sold the rug to a dealer who sold it at auction for $1,000.

On another occasion while in New York City, he bought twenty-five oil paintings tied together with string for about $50, convinced that he could sell them for the frames alone and earn back his money. When he was unpacking the pictures at his warehouse in Dallas, the husband of one of his customers came by and shouted, "Lee, Lee, you've got Onderdonks."

"Step on them," said Lee, thinking of some heaven-knows-what he had picked up in his travels from New York to Dallas.

"No, no, you don't understand," said the man. "You've bought Onderdonks." Lee had bought a collection of paintings by one Julian Onderdonk, an artist who had lived in New York but moved to Texas. There he be-

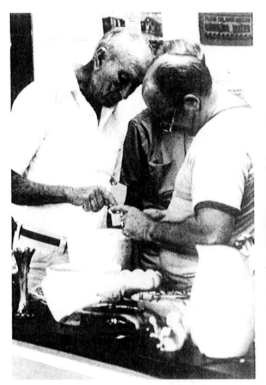 

came well known as one of the "Blue Bonnet" painters, because of his many paintings of the cornflower, or blue bonnet, the state flower of Texas.

Box lots don't often have such Jack-in-the-box surprises, but they are worth looking at.

### Repairing Imperfections and Other Problems

Now let's say you've seen and thoroughly examined a wonderful small table at the exhibition. It would be perfect to put in your hallway so you'd have a place to rest your packages, but one leg is very loose and would have to be repaired. You see that the table is put together with dowels; trying to repair it by hammering in a nail or

using glue would definitely spoil it. You know that you're buying it as is, of course, and that any repairs would be your responsibility and your expense.

This is a fairly typical occurrence at auctions, and since repair or restoration costs detract from what might otherwise be an excellent buy, a necessary component of "know-before-you-go" is learning about repair costs before you bid. One way to find out about these costs is to have a specialist examine the item and give you an estimate.

Understandably, repairers and restorers object to being asked to give their time and expert advice without receiving any recompense, since their income is directly related to the time they are actually working. Time away from their work is almost literally money lost. If you are a regular customer and they know you will give them the repair job if you buy the item, there is little difficulty. The

## Learning About Repairs

*More and more local colleges, continuing-education departments, and museums are offering courses in how to repair used furniture, antiques, paintings, and so on, simply because more and more of us are buying at auction. It might pay you to learn what is being offered in your area that could give you some expertise in repairing. If there is no course, you might approach your local schools, colleges, or adult-education centers, and ask if they would consider setting one up.*

*The more you know about such skills, the more you will be able to discuss a particular problem intelligently with the experts. And you'll be in a fine position to judge whether the person understands the problem and can deal with it, and if the estimate you've been given is a fair one.*

repair mastercraftsman will inspect the piece and give you an estimate on the costs, including approximate prices of the materials needed (handles, upholstery fabrics, special paints), at no charge.

What if you're not a regular customer? Then the repairer will usually be willing to give you an estimate for a stated fee, which might include both the actual inspection and the travel time. If this is the arrangement you make, ask to have the fee deducted from the repair charge if you do give the person the job. Customarily craftsmen will agree to this.

Since the demand for skilled artisans and craftsmen far exceeds the supply, it will pay you to establish a good relationship with this much-sought-after, almost-vanishing breed of individuals. Some auction houses have lists of movers, repairers, and restorers that they will share with you. They usually don't make recommendations, since they are loath to get into what can be a very tricky business, but they will, as a service, offer you names and addresses.

What about other possible problems that might need a

specialist? Brass handles or brass mounts on furniture can be badly tarnished or corroded; unfortunately, they can't be cleaned with ordinary brass cleaners. Gold-leaf mirrors or picture frames require skilled restoration. Old rugs usually cannot be trusted to an ordinary rug cleaner, but in most cases should be cleaned by a specialist.

Despite the cost of having this special work done, you may still—as you well know if you've shopped for furniture or rugs recently—get a better mirror, or rug, or piece of furniture by buying an antique than by buying an equivalent new piece. But you should at least get some ideas of the cost (and the travail) of buying anything that needs restoration.

97

## Repairs And Restoration— Much More Than Meets The Eye

*I want to pass on to you the frequent complaint of expert restorers that customers don't appreciate the problems of restoring or repairing. Every expert furniture restorer can cite with horror the customer who shows him a piece of furniture, a table for instance, and says, "It probably needs just a little bracing, or glue, or a few screws here and there. How much will it cost?" When the expert says, "Several hundred dollars," the innocent but ignorant customer looks at him as if he has just committed an unspeakable crime.*

*According to one expert in the field, Michael Varese, here are just some of the items a good restorer of antique furniture should know in order to do a good job. He should know something about the methods of constructing an antique piece of furniture, so that he could duplicate them or take the piece apart if necessary. He should then be able to reassemble it, either in the old way or in a new way that would not be clearly visible. He should also know something about the character of wood—for instance, that wood often shrinks across its width but not its length. (Just imagine an old plank that gets narrower but not shorter, says Mr. Varese.) He should know how to remove old dirt and polish because if they are not removed properly, the new piece will not adhere properly. If braces are needed, he should know how they can be recessed to make them invisible. He should know how to clean the old finish without cleaning it so thoroughly that it looks as if it's brand new and not an antique.*

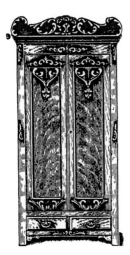

*Which will give you some sense of the task often facing restorers.*

All of this brings up the logical question: Should you buy furniture that's already been repaired? Many veteran auction-goers say no, you should not. The reasons? You really don't know what you're getting and you may just be buying a headache. You don't know how good the

98

repair is, how well it was done, or how long it will last. Furthermore, precisely because such comments are standard advice, it is difficult to resell things that have been repaired, especially furniture.

However, from my point of view as someone who likes to buy for use and enjoyment rather than to acquire a museum piece or an investment, I think this advice has to be tempered somewhat, depending on what you are buying, the quality of the repair, what you intend to do with the piece—and above all, the price.

So far we've considered how you can become knowledgeable about the goods coming up for sale. But you also need to know about the auction house doing the selling. So we'll take a look at that next.

# 6 MORE TO KNOW BEFORE YOU GO: ABOUT THE AUCTION HOUSE

Auction-goers soon learn that different auction houses often have slightly different ways of doing business, starting with whether they designate themselves an auction "house," "gallery," or "barn," or simply go by their corporate name. Your life as an auction-goer will be easier if you know more about these differences.

*How You Pay*

Let's start with that fundamental of fundamentals: money. Even though you don't pay until you actually offer the winning bid, you should know, before the first item goes on the block, just how you would be expected to pay for it. What are the requirements of an auction house when it comes to money, particularly cash versus credit?

*100*

- Cash is always acceptable, or that almost-cash equivalent, traveler's checks. (Some of us are so accustomed to reaching for a plastic card that it's almost a shock to find there are places where cash is not only acceptable but actually welcome.)
- Some auction houses will take credit cards—but many will not.
- Some will accept a personal check with proper identification, unless it is for a large sum (hundreds of dollars or more). Some will take checks only if you establish credit far enough in advance for the auction house to run a credit check on you.
- Some will not allow you to remove your merchandise until the check has cleared, that is, has been accepted by the bank on which it was drawn. (If you have made a successful absentee bid, the auction house will not send you the merchandise until the check has cleared.)
- Some will insist on a certified check or cashier's check, that is, a check with a guarantee from the bank that funds are available.

Obviously, you'll want to be prepared by having on hand whatever kind of money or money substitute the auction house requires. If you have any questions about the house's money policy, a simple phone call will quickly bring you the answer.

*How You Become a Bidder*

What do you need if you want to bid? Some auction houses require only that you come and bid. In such instances, if you are a successful bidder, an employee approaches you wherever you are sitting or standing, and fills out a form with the information the house needs: your name, address, the lot number, and so on.

Some houses ask you to register and take a number, which may be on a paddle (which looks something like a Ping-Pong paddle), or a numbered card, or the back of a paper plate. Don't feel foolish if you think the paddle number is a seat number; it's a common mistake at auctions.

Some ask you not only to register and take a number, but also to put down a deposit, which may range from $5 to $50. This deposit is refundable when you leave if you don't buy anything. Other auction houses don't require a deposit but *suggest* that you make one (refundable, of course). Then, they say, if you are the successful bidder, all you need to do when approached by a floor aide is to say that you have a deposit, rather than stopping to answer the questions on the bidding form and perhaps missing the opportunity to bid on other things.

Perfectly true, and sometimes to be considered. On the other hand, you should also consider the psychological aspect of the deposit. What you have done, in effect, is given yourself "permission" to spend. Unconsciously, you can now easily say to yourself, "What the hell, I've already laid out the money, so why not go ahead and bid for something." The suggested deposit is auction "advice" that I would handle with care.

*How You Get Your Goods*

Let's say you have bid successfully. What next? Where do you get your purchases? At times you pick them up all at once, when you are ready to leave. Depending on the size of the auction house, there may be two places (and at a busy auction, sometimes two lines of people waiting): an office where you pay and another place where you pick up your purchase. Sometimes there are signs and/or announcements indicating where you pay and where you pick up, sometimes there aren't. (The lack of signs is one of my complaints about auction houses. There's nothing more annoying than waiting in the wrong line.) If the office or cashier is not clearly marked, ask as you go into the auction house.

At on-site house auctions, the auctioneer will usually

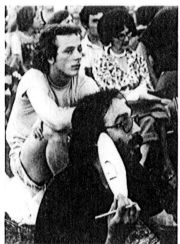

announce the rules of the day at the start of the auction, which is fine for the earlybirds, but not much help if you come later. At these auctions, the cashiers sit in a very prominent spot—to give numbers to newcomers, to collect a deposit if it's a requirement for bidding, and just generally to keep an eye on the proceedings. But you may save yourself some time and annoyance if you ask, as you come in, where to pick up and where to pay. Sometimes, at informal auctions, an employee will simply hand you your purchase or purchases, and it's taken for granted that you will pay for them later. (There is trust and faith at these auctions—and also you *have* given your name and address when you've been given a number.)

If you've been the successful bidder for several items, especially small ones, you will do well to keep a record of the lot numbers of your bids. Then you can check the bookkeeper's tally at the end of the auction, or when you go to pick up your purchases.

Auctions are fast-moving operations and, unless very expensive items are being auctioned, the house is under great pressure to move quickly. The faster and the more

### The Movable Feast of House Parts

*Perhaps the ultimate test of transporting things from an auction took place at the auction of Mohican Manor, a Federal-style mansion on Lake Oneanta in New York state. It had been the summer house of the Spaulding family and was sold literally piece by piece: door by door, fixture by fixture, staircase, foundation stones, cisterns, everything. More than 1500 people came from all over the United States: dealers, restaurant owners, disco and nightclub owners, and private individuals. Over a period of two and a half weeks, the house was demolished. Auctioneers Richard C. Gilbert and his father, O. Rundle Gilbert, worked their way down the house floor by floor, selling marble-top sinks; cast iron and enamel bathtubs; standard-sized bedroom doors; oversized reception-room doors; shield-shaped windows with carved moldings.*

*After the stairways were sold, customers had to use ladders to get their purchases. The successful bidders came with trucks, heavy tools, and chain saws, and had to be carefully supervised so that removing their doors, floors, beams, or parts of staircases didn't bring the remainder of the house tumbling down. One of the more spectacular jobs was removing part of the peaked roof, which was destined to be added to the house of Mrs. Helen Dillon, part owner of the New York Jets football team. Her share of the roof was sawed off with a chain saw and then lifted away with a crane.*

casual the auction, the better off you are picking up your purchases quickly, especially box lots. By saying this, I am in no way impugning the integrity of auctioneers or their employees, though there are angels and devils among them, as elsewhere in life. It's just that they don't always have time or, often, sufficient staff to pay attention to which piece fell out of which lot.

It's this same pressure of limited time and limited storage space that forces auction houses to have rigid rules about removing purchases. Usually, you are required to pick up your purchases either immediately or within a time limit of a few days. If you don't, the house may reserve the right to charge you for storage in their own space, to remove your purchases to a public storage house and charge you for that, or to resell your property at auction and keep all or part of the proceeds. Some of these fine-print provisions may never have been tested in a court of law, and no one can say definitively that the auctioneer's right to take these actions has been proven. Nevertheless, part of your buying plans should be a provision for getting your lucky finds home safely and quickly.

### *"Guesstimating" the Prices*

When you go to the presale exhibition, you'll want to make a note of the presale estimates. If it's a catalog sale, the figures will probably be in the catalog, sometimes along with the descriptions of individual items, sometimes on separate pages in the back of the catalog. Even if it's a noncatalog sale, the auction house may have presale estimates on posted lists you can consult. If you don't see them, ask if they're available. And if there are no presale estimates, ask employees on the floor, or the auctioneer, what they estimate a piece will bring.

Why do you want to know this? You may be able to judge whether it is or isn't within your price range. If you're very knowledgeable, you may recognize an unusual piece that is worth more than the presale estimate indicates, which means you want to be sure that you are there to bid. You also want time to think about how much you are willing to pay to get it. You may look at the presale estimates and decide that they are, in general, too high, and that you need to be very wary when bidding—or that it's one sale you might just want to skip.

Some auctioneers are very strongly opposed to presale estimates and reserves and don't allow them at their auctions. They consider such practices an unfair arrangement, by the consignor and the auctioneer, to set higher prices. These auctioneers believe that the price set by open bidding at the auction is the *only* equitable price. It is an interesting and certainly valid point of view. If the auction is an open market, anything that presets the price takes away from that open competition. (Of course, as you'll see in later chapters, the consignor has a different opinion, and the auctioneer is caught somewhere in the middle, since he has to satisfy both buyer and seller.)

Many auction houses don't have presale estimates simply because their auctions are too informal to attempt such estimates. This is especially true of the casual consignment auctions, where local people bring in whatever they want to sell, and take whatever they can get. (I asked one auctioneer what she did with the things that didn't sell—the beyond-repair old furniture, toys, broken strings of beads—and she laughed and said when the auction's over, they "take them out back and bury them.")

Some auction houses print a list of the final "knockdown" prices and will mail you the list if you ask. (There may be a small—$2 to $3—fee.) This can be a very good way of getting a "feel" for current market prices.

*Knowing the Final Total Price*

You will also want to find out if the auction charges a buyer's "premium," customarily ten percent. Note that I've put that word "premium" in quotes. The primary dictionary definition of *premium* is a "prize," "bonus," or "reward." But a "buyer's premium" at an auction is no prize for you. Instead, it's the auction industry's euphemism for a buyer's *fee*.

Unfortunately, this ten percent buyer's premium is increasingly being adopted by auction houses around the country. It's a charge that's announced in the catalog, on

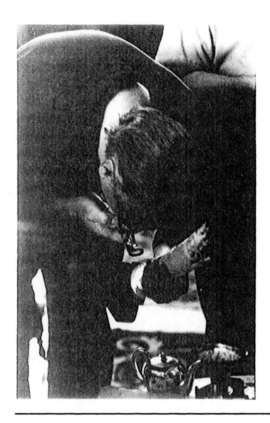

signs at the auction gallery, and/or by the auctioneer at the time of the auction. If you're not sure, ask. When you bid, you want to know if you're going to have to pay another ten percent in addition to the final knock-down price.

Other possible costs: If you live in a state with a sales tax, the auctioneer is responsible for collecting it. And if you live in a state that requires sterilization of upholstered furniture, you may have to pay for that, too.

*The Auction-Goer's Grab Bag of Advance Tips*

Now let's get down to some bedrock details that will make your life as an auction-goer just that much easier:

107

things you should carry with you, have in your car, wear, plan ahead for—in short, advance preparation "kits" (literally and figuratively). The first items are fairly clear-cut:

1. Paper and pencils or pens—they seem obvious, until you find you don't have them! So don't forget to bring pens or pencils and a notebook or small pad on which you can list the catalog or lot number and the pre-sale estimates of the goods you want to bid on. You might even write down your upper limit for each item, just so you won't forget and also to help you ward off attacks of auction fever (which dread virus we'll examine in Chapter Seven).

2. Take along at least one and perhaps two flashlights: a pen-sized light for looking into small vases or small holes to check for defects; and a larger one for looking into drawers and closets in larger pieces of furniture. Auction exhibition space is often quite dim, and you really need these lights if you're going to inspect something thoroughly. And at the risk of repeating myself, I will do just that and say again that you must examine everything painstakingly: open drawers, test knobs, look at all sides of the furniture, lift the cushions, crawl under the piano.

3. Invest in a good yardstick and tape measure. Use them to check the dimensions of the space you plan to fill at your home or office, and also to measure furniture at the auction, to be sure things will fit. And don't forget to measure the dimensions of your car, van, or station wagon, so you're sure of what you can and cannot haul.

4. Consider investing in a portable ultraviolet lamp, useful for revealing what is not otherwise visible, including restorations, repairs, overpainting, added and fake signatures, counterfeits, imperfections, even dirt in crevices. Different varieties of such lamps are available from laboratory supply houses and some rock supply stores. (Yes, rock supply stores.)

5. Take along packing materials, such as string, rope,

A Useful
Minilamp

*Michael Filides, a Boston antique dealer, has invented a portable minilamp that's about as big as a paperback book (6 x 3½ x 1 inches) and weighs less than four ounces. The lamp is useful for revealing repairs, restorations, imperfections, and so on.*

*Mr. Filides told me he did this almost in desperation, to ease his task in his buying trips around the world. His minilamp has been bought by many of the major auction houses. It's available by mail for about $43. Write to Nordest, 206 Newbury Street, Boston, Massachusetts 02116.*

twine, old newspapers, tissue paper, plastic bags, shopping bags, old blankets or quilts, plus a knife or scissors. Some auction houses will wrap for you; others will not. Wrapping is usually a courtesy of the house, not something that's required. And it's at your own risk. So it pays to have your own supplies to be sure that you get your goodies home safely.

6. Take along a magnifying glass—very useful for looking at tiny identifying marks on silver (for example, the word *sterling*), and on china, glass, and pottery.

7. Take along a printed price guide, or several if you have more than one. Some auction aficionados say to take along *all* your guides, but to me that seems burdensome. However, it does pay to have them at home, for the things you are interested in buying and/or collecting. The guides are limited, admittedly, because prices are continually changing, but at least they offer a standard against which to evaluate presale estimates, and give some indication of the state of the market.

For instance, when we decided to sell an antique gold man's pocket watch, I checked first in the current edition of *Antiques and Other Collectibles,* by Grace McFarland, to see the range of prices for such watches. Although the guide didn't list the exact watch we owned, it listed several that seemed similar. The prices gave me some idea about the value of the watch and a basis for judging other watches that I saw at auction, and, later, for evaluating the fairness of the estimates auctioneers and dealers quoted.

8. Take along a magnet, which will attract iron but not solid copper, bronze, or brass.

9. If you think you might buy some furniture that will require moving by truck, think about how you would arrange it. Many auction houses have movers that they will refer you to—but with the understanding that they are not making a recommendation, simply a referral. (The auction house doesn't want to be responsible in any way for the arrangements. That's between you and the mover.) In addition to local movers, you might also consider a local gardener, if it's the winter when they're not so busy. Other sources are your local colleges, which often have student employment offices, or the Yellow Pages of your telephone directory. Of course, if you have bought an antique that requires special handling, you'll want a mover with that kind of experience. Whatever your source for movers, it's a good idea to check ahead of time on how they will charge, by the hour or flat fee, and how they want to be paid, by cash or check.

*More Advance Tips*

The next items are more personal and so more varied.

Let's start with food. Many auctioneers do not break for lunch. If you don't want to leave and perhaps miss an item that interests you, bring your own—if not lunch, at least a snack. Other auctions, especially country auctions, will have food available; very often it's a fund-raising activity for the local women's club, or wives' auxiliary, or the firemen's association. (However, their idea of lunch or snacks may not be yours. Hot dogs are the favorite from coast to coast, plus fattening snacks, such as potato chips, french fries, doughnuts, cookies. I believe there is a fortune to be made by the person who starts a fresh-fruit-and-vegetable nibbles concession at auctions.)

The informality of country auctions—particularly those held out-of-doors—is important in other ways, too. For example, seating is not guaranteed at many country auctions. It pays to have along a blanket or beach towel, folding chairs or stools, unless you don't mind sitting on the grass.

Weather is one of the unpredictables at outdoor auctions, much to the despair of auctioneers. A beautiful sunny day can turn cloudy, cool, or, worst of all, rainy and windy. It's good to bring a sweater or jacket, especially for those auctions that start late in the day and go on into the evening, when there's a good chance the weather will be much cooler.

Shoes are also important at country auctions, especially the small auctions where good bargains can be found. You may walk around in mud if it's rained recently, or dirt. You may have to jump up onto a fairly high loading platform to get into the main auction room; or the seats may be built stadium-style and you may have to climb rather rickety steps to get to the upper rows. Low-heeled comfortable shoes or boots are best.

At almost any auction, you might find it a good idea to wear something bright—a red blouse or yellow shirt. It's useful at auctions where they don't use bidding cards or paddles. I've heard the auctioneer at New York City galleries say, "Sold to the lady in red," or "Sold to the gentleman in the yellow shirt."

Sun hats are great complexion-savers and sunburn-protectors at outdoor auctions.

Many outdoor house auctions use those practical but smelly, claustrophobic Port-O-San toilet facilities. Be sure that, like all experienced travelers, you have your own supply of tissues and those packaged mini washcloths. (To be very practical—if you have a sensitive nose—take along a clothespin to use as a nose-pincher.)

Should you bring your children? Auctioneers are not

naturally mean or misanthropic; many of them are parents, and many auction houses are family affairs. But auctioneers don't like children at auctions. Babies sometimes cry just when the bidding is getting "hot"; small children like to run up and down the aisles or play with the dolls and toys that may be part of the sale. So note if the advertisement of an auction says "No Children" and act accordingly. Sometimes it means they really won't be admitted; sometimes they have to sit in the back away from the main seating area; sometimes it's okay if they play outside the auction house—but they often need to be watched since tools and other equipment are sometimes left there, to say nothing of the cars and motorcycles coming and going in the parking lot.

No need to be unyieldingly rigid on this point. At some country auctions, you'll see babies and young children, and no one will say a word. But in general, auctions are for adults, not kids. They have their games; we have ours.

All this advance preparation frees you to enjoy a day at the auction, secure, even nonchalant, in the comfort of knowing you're well prepared. You can concentrate on getting the best buys, having the most fun—and acquiring, whether or not you do buy, some satisfying memories.

But now that we're so primed to enjoy ourselves, you naturally want to know: How do we actually participate? How does a person *bid*?

That's our next topic.

# 7    **HOW TO BID**

To bid at an auction for the first time is to be full of doubt and a bit of stage fright. All those stories you've heard about scratching your ear or tucking in a stray wisp of hair and finding that you just bought a chest of drawers! Are they true? No. But it is true that you'll probably suffer from stage fright, and you'll discover you're somewhat afraid of the sound of your own voice in a quiet room, or feel a little foolish about bidding for something whose value you don't know for a fact. It may even cross your mind to wonder if people think you're cheap if you buy a set of used silverware, though you know it will be completely sanitary when you get it home and wash it.

Be consoled—all of us who have bid at an auction had exactly those feelings the first time, and they really don't matter. You can be sure you'll get accustomed to bidding, even though the sweaty palms and fast heartbeat may never go away entirely, especially if you're bidding for something you want badly.

However, there are ways and ways of bidding. So let's talk about how to bid to your best advantage.

### Doing Your Homework

First, a quick review of what you should have done to prepare yourself. You've gone to the presale exhibition or, if there was none, you've arrived at the auction early enough to rummage around among the boxes, and to examine—carefully!—any paintings, equipment, furniture, lamps, and so on that interest you.

You've bought a catalog or picked up the list of lots, which may or may not include the estimated prices at which they will be sold. If there are no presale estimates, and you're especially interested in a particular item, you may have asked the auctioneer what he thinks the piece will go for. (Remember, the auctioneer is not always the best authority since, consciously or unconsciously, he has a vested interest in not giving too low a price.)

You've inquired about the rules of the auction house. Do you need a paddle to bid? A number? Must you register in advance and pay a fee, refunded if you don't buy? It's important to get these rules clear. You don't want to bid on something only to lose it, or slow up the auction and have everyone looking at you in annoyance because you didn't have a number.

You've set for yourself a dollar limit on the items that you want, and like many experienced auction-goers, you've written that limit in your catalog. (It serves as a reminder to you that you have an upper limit, and helps develop an immunity to auction fever.)

If you're worried during your first few auctions that the auctioneer won't see you, you've decided to sit close to the front. You may even have decided to wear a bright dress or shirt, so you really can't be missed.

You've probably already noticed a group of men and women who usually sit or stand near each other, very often at the back of the room. They may very well be dealers—friendly competitors. They are sometimes a noisy group, joking, laughing, walking around, ducking out for smokes, but never missing the bids on the items they want. Should you sit near them? Maybe, in the beginning, just to see how they act, what they bid on. But, because they are noisy, they can distract you. Furthermore, they are usually known to the auctioneer because they are regular customers. He watches for their sometimes prearranged signals, and may overlook your bids. So you are better off sitting some distance from them.

Okay—your homework is out of the way. What now? Time to settle back and observe the auctioneer.

115

*The Auctioneer's Spiel*

Depending on the section of the country, the tradition of a particular auction house, and the taste of the individual auctioneer, the style of auctioneering will vary, and so will the auctioneer's accents or tone. (I'm going to talk about "him" but it could just as easily be "her," since more and more women are becoming auctioneers.)

Their different accents won't matter much to you, but it's fun to be aware of them. At the big urban auction galleries, especially those that are offshoots of the English houses, the tone is very apt to be upper-class, English or American. For instance, the auctioneer will speak like this: "I now have $200 from the gentleman on my left, $225 from the gentleman on my right. Now it's your bid, Madam, at $250." And so on.

At other houses in different areas around the country, you could hear a midwestern twang, a New England broad *A* or a trace of New York or Brooklyn. The auctioneer may also use the auctioneer's chant—that is, give the advancing bids in a continuous rhythmic chant interspersed with "filler" words that may have no meaning but serve to keep the rhythm going. It might sound something like this: "Twenty-five bid hoola gimme [who will give me] 30; 30 bid hoola gimme 35," and so on. The chant keeps the bidding continuous, adds excitement, and maintains the fast pace that the auctioneer hopes will induce people to get in and bid. Auctioneers who like this method (it's a carryover from cattle auctions) take great pride in how fast they can chant, and have annual competitions to see who can chant most rapidly and intelligibly.

Note that *intelligibly.* Here we come to the more substantive aspects of an auctioneer's style. For your purposes, you don't care if the auctioneer's accent is straight from London, New London, or old St. Louis. What you do care about is that you understand the dollar price, and a good auctioneer should make this very plain.

116

You also want to understand the increments, that is, the dollar amounts by which the prices are being increased. Is it $5, $10, $25 or, in very high-class auctions, even $1000? You have to know this and you also need to observe carefully what happens as the auctioneer, after starting the bid, continues the increments, since it is his prerogative to change them.

A good auctioneer will periodically "bring in the handle" so that you do know what's going on. For instance, the bidding may go something like this: "I'm bid 100, now 25; do you want it at 25? 25, now 50, do you want it at 50? 50, will you make it 75? I'm bid 150, now 75, will you make it 75? Do you want it at 75? I'm bid 175; will you bid 200?" Notice that the auctioneer, besides giving the increments (in this case $25), is also telling you what the total is—he is "bringing in the handle" so that you know you're not bidding $25 or $50 or $75, but $125 or $250 or $275. (The word *dollar* is usually mentioned only occasionally since it's taken for granted that everyone understands the bids are in dollars.)

The auctioneer may also *jump* the bid, that is, he may start at $10 then go to $25, then $35, then $50, then $60, then $75, then $85, and then $100. Obviously, he has a great advantage in doing it this way. It takes the same amount of time to get a higher price—if the audience goes along. Let's say he's been advancing the bids by $10: $110, then $120, then $130, at which point he says $145. If no one is interested at $145, he can always drop it back to $140. But if someone does say $145, the auctioneer has won his little gamble, and he can then ask for $160. From $160 he can jump to $175, and from there, if the bidding is lively, to $200.

You have something to say about increments too. There are two signals for indicating that you want to cut the going price in half. One is done by tucking your thumb under the palm of your hand, and then slicing the air in front of you, meaning that if the current increment is ten dollars you want to halve that increment to five

How to Be
A Mystery
Bidder

*If you prefer to bid anonymously, you can, as long as you and the auctioneer have arranged your signals in advance. Some dealers like to remain anonymous, on the theory that anyone who sees they are interested in a painting, for instance, will naturally assume that the painting has value and so may bid against the dealer, raising the price.*

*You may have your own reasons for not wanting to be identified: You may be leery of getting known as a collector and then being approached by dealers. You may not want it known that you are the owner of something valuable. You may just be a very private person.*

*Whatever the reason, you can work it out with the auctioneer. One New Jersey auctioneer has an arrangement with one of his customers to reverse the side of the room. This customer likes to bid by raising one of his index fingers. But when he does, and he's sitting to the auctioneer's left, the auctioneer says (while looking directly at the customer) "The bid is now on my right at X dollars." This works for them, because they have prearranged it, and understand each other.*

dollars. Let's say the bidding for a vase had been forty dollars, then fifty, then sixty. You enter the bid with the half signal, which means you are bidding but you want to bid only sixty-five, not seventy. As always, the auctioneer has the option of refusing this lowering of the increment. If he accepts, bids advance from that point on by five dollars not ten.

The other signal is crossing one index finger over the other, which also indicates you want to cut the increment in half. The result is the same as the "slice-the-air" signal.

One auctioneer, Colonel K. R. French, in a throwaway he distributes at his auctions, describes an auction this way: "The true definition of an auction is a public sale by public outcry to gain for the seller the highest price pos-

sible, by open and fair competitive bidding, free from all forms of chicanery, monkey business, and crookedness of all kinds. At auctions you like tó buy items as cheap as possible and I want to sell them as high as possible. Hopefully we can meet somewhere in the middle without getting mad." So, you don't have to get "mad" when the auctioneer jumps the bid, but you don't have to follow his lead either.

I've been at auctions when the auctioneer asked for $20 and when he got it, jumped to $40, then a bidder quietly said $30. It's the auctioneer's prerogative to accept or refuse this lower bid; and if the bidding is slow, auctioneers are likely to accept it. Obviously, it doesn't always happen this way, but it's always your option to try a

119

lower bid, just as it's the auctioneer's option not to accept it. An auction is a contest, and as bidders we want to be the winners.

It's also *very* important that you understand exactly how the auctioneer is defining what you are bidding for. These are various ways an auctioneer can sell items that he has grouped together, and these differences seriously affect your potential purchases.

For instance, an auctioneer can combine several items together in a lot and offer it under the rubric "choice with privilege." What does this mean? Let's say three quite similar cut-glass pitchers are being sold at the same time. "Choice with privilege" means that if you make the successful bid, you have the privilege of choosing which of the three pitchers you want. After you have made your choice, the other two pitchers will go back on the block.

Another option on grouped items may be "by the piece." Let's say, for instance, that there are twenty similar Italian pottery dishes. If you win the bid "by the piece," you can take either any one of them or as many as you want, paying for each the price you bid. (Sometimes there will be a small minimum number you must take.)

A third choice might be by the piece, but you must take the lot. This means that the *price* of each item is set by the bid on the individual piece but you must buy all the items, the entire lot.

If you have doubt as to the terms of the pieces you are bidding for—whether you must take one, ten or a hundred—don't be bashful. Call out and ask the auctioneer, or ask one of the employees of the gallery who is on the floor. Or, if you can't find out, don't bid, since you are responsible for knowing this should you become the successful bidder.

Boyd Michael, an auctioneer, a registrar at the Missouri Auction School, and an authority on cattle, likes to tell how he learned to make clear to an audience the terms under which they were bidding. As a beginning auctioneer, he was selling 2000 bales of hay. A little old lady in the audience was bidding avidly and ended up as the successful bidder. He said "Two thousand bales of hay to number fifty," and the poor woman looked aghast. She thought she had been bidding for one bale for her pet rabbit. Mr. Michael opted to start the bidding all over. After that experience, he says, he never forgot to explain precisely what people were bidding for when there was more than one piece in a lot.

*Putting Your Best Bid Forward*

Now it's your turn. If you're bidding for the first time, you may be tempted, as soon as the auctioneer announces the opening price, to accept his suggested price as your bid. Most seasoned auction-goers (and auctioneers speaking off the record) say this is a mistake. Remember that the auctioneer likes to start the bidding at a price which he estimates will be at least close to the final price at which the piece will be sold. It's also to his advantage, within the range of reasonableness, to start the bidding at a good price. He has little to lose since he can always go down. So why should the first bidder start at this high price? It's better to have the bids begin at a low price which the auctioneer may or may not accept. The audience can always go higher if the auctioneer refuses the first bid.

For obvious reasons, auction-goers and dealers don't like the naive person who, attending his or her first auction, is so anxious to get something that the person overbids. Listen to this comment from a collectors' newsletter about an auction of photographs: "There are a large number of new buyers. This encouraging fact was marked by the usual excessive enthusiasm that causes these neophytes to bid currently available material far above estimates and gallery prices. . . . The far-reaching effect of overbidding is to drive prices upward on a mis-

taken assumption, perhaps not unrelated to certain avaricious tendencies, that this bidding comes as a result of increased general demand, when actually it comes from . . . uninformed sporting types finding themselves competing in the same game." You, of course, don't want to be one of these "uninformed sporting types" who drive up the prices.

A better time for you to make your move, if the opportunity presents itself, is when the bidding slows down on a series of objects. At this point it's up to the auctioneer to get it going again. He may tell a few jokes, he may ring a cowbell or two. "We just wanted to wake up the audience." He may group a few lots together (called "pyramiding") for one price. He may offer a few items again at a low price—anything to get the bidding going again. It's at moments like this, when the rhythm slackens and the auctioneer begins to worry, that you can pick up some

## Farewell, Again, To Judy Garland

*Some auctions are filled with nostalgia and sadness. If you had been a Judy Garland fan, for instance, you would have wanted to go to the 1978 auction of some of her possessions, put on the block by Sid Luft, the third of her five husbands. The auction was held in the grand ballroom of the very grand Beverly Wilshire Hotel in Beverly Hills, California, where the rich, elite, and famous come to shop and be seen at the superexpensive shops on Rodeo Drive.*

*Mr. Luft, in his sixties, decided about nine years after her death to auction off some five hundred mementos of Miss Garland's movie career and their life together. Included were such items as: a white leather and brass chair from the beach house in* A Star Is Born; *the lucite coffee table on which she danced in the same movie; a pair of Miss Garland's false eyelashes and eyebrows, plus an eyelash curler; the silver thermos she kept at her bedside; a leather-bound book of poetry she wrote, entitled* Thoughts and Poetry by Judy Garland; *Judy's queen-sized bed, topped by a hand-carved, three-section love seat converted into a headboard, with pure-silk upholstered panels and hand-carved gilt decorations of grapes and leaves on an antique-white background; Miss Garland's own copy of Moss Hart's first draft of* A Star Is Born; *a pair of loaded dice given her by her neighbor, Humphrey Bogart, at the start of the filming of* A Star *(he had used them in* Casablanca); *the cane she used when she sang "Swanee," one of the many songs that brought the house down in* A Star.

*If you had been a really devoted fan, afraid you might not get in, you would have paid $100 to a scalper for a reserved seat that the auction house, the C. B. Charles' Galleries, had sold for $25. Before taking your seat, you would have browsed among the memorabilia: Judy's sequined gowns and pants; her golf clubs; a tiny porcelain piano she had kept on a mantel in her New York apartment; photos of Judy during her forty* ☛

*years in show business. And while you browsed, clips from her movies were flashing on a screen and her voice was resounding from the ballroom's speakers.*

*Then you would have joined about five hundred fans, movie stars, collectors, and a few dealers who gathered under the immense crystal chandeliers of the ballroom. (Mr. Luft had chosen the ballroom for the auction, despite its cost of $7,500 for two days, because "Judy should have a beautiful setting.") To your left, there could have been an admirer with a carefully hoarded $75 in her wallet and a Judy picture-pin on her dress. To your right, perhaps, Jane Withers, the actress. Or perhaps an agent for Lily Tomlin, who couldn't be there. She bought the loaded dice Judy had received from Humphrey Bogart.*

*The last item to be sold, at the evening session that went on until after midnight, was Miss Garland's 1953 black Mercedes-Benz coupe, plus a set of matched pigskin luggage. The "package" went for $60,000, seven times the original cost of the car.*

real bargains. At an auction there seem to be waves of interest and then lulls, perhaps because of the heat or the hour or because people are hungry or because many people are interested in only one particular part of the auction. So it's worthwhile to pay attention to how fast the bidding is going. When it's going slowly, you may get a bargain.

Don't be shy in calling out your first bid loud and clear, so the auctioneer sees immediately that you are interested. Ordinarily you needn't worry about being overlooked. Part of an auctioneer's training is to be adept at scanning the room and noticing everyone who is interested in bidding. Furthermore, even at very small auctions, there are people working with the auctioneer to help "spot" bidders. (They're sometimes known as "ring men," from the livestock auctions where men were liter-

ally in the ring with the animals, both to prod them into view and to help the auctioneer spot the bidders.) And at the biggest auctions, when the audience may be in main and side rooms, employees in contact with the auctioneer are always in the side rooms to report the bids from there. (Million-dollar bidders get invited to the main room at the next special auction!)

But what if the auctioneer does pass over your bid, which does sometimes happen. What should you do? It's possible that he either didn't see you or didn't hear you, especially if the room is noisy or you're partially obscured by someone in front of you. Again, faint heart never won fair prize at auction. Say your bid loudly again, and if you still aren't noticed holler! Say "I'm in" or "How about me?" or "I am interested"—something along these lines.

Don't treat being passed over as a slight. The auctioneer relies on his public image to develop and maintain both his reputation and that of his auction house. He wants to be known as being above "monkey business" and "chicanery," to use Colonel French's words. You can and should take advantage of this. Most auctioneers are honest and are not out to cheat their customers, if for no other reason than that it's bad for business. (Of course, there are always occasional incidents of auctioneers who are in collusion with a particular gallery, or dealer, or even a private buyer. That's a different problem, not relevant for our purposes here.) If you really want something, speak up or make sure that the auctioneer sees your private signal.

Once you have started bidding and are really interested, the auctioneer will keep his eye on you. At this point it's to your advantage to bid quickly because the auctioneer will pay attention to you rather than scan the audience for other possible bidders. If the auction is fast-moving, this ploy will help freeze out the competition. Remember that the essence of an auction is the quick decision, especially if the auctioneer has a large assortment of pieces to auction. An auctioneer will try to maintain a pace of sixty to one hundred lots an hour. Serious bidders don't let themselves get distracted by chatting with friends until they have either won the bid or chosen to drop out.

So far we've covered some basic guidelines. Now what about those "code" ways of bidding you hear so much about? Is this something that should concern you? Is there a special bidding style you should develop?

Many people do have amusing and different styles of bidding. Peter Fairbanks, a senior vice-president of Phillips in New York, has a long list of bidding classifications, among them: the flagger, the snapper, the snap-and-stare-hard-at-your-adversary, the steady hand, the friendly wave, the deep stare, the earlobe tickler, and the hollerer. Dealers in particular like to develop individual styles—waving an unlit cigar, tugging on a beard, a just

126

## Those *Very* Airy "Air" Bids

*No discussion of bidding would be complete without mentioning what is delicately known in the trade as "air bids." You'll notice sometimes that the auctioneer will wave his hand in the air in the general direction of the audience and say "I have 25," or "Fifty bid, will you make it 60?" Don't bother to crane your neck to see who is bidding—no one is. The air bid is a ploy auctioneers use to get the bidding going when the audience is sitting on its hands on a sultry day, or sometimes to cut off a customer who is trying to change the increments.*

*Suppose, for instance, that the bid on a cut glass bowl has been advancing by $25 increments and the price is up to $200. The auctioneer says, "I'm bid 200, do I hear 225?" and someone in the audience offers $210. The auctioneer doesn't want to refuse the $210, but he doesn't want to accept it if he doesn't have to. So he points to a spot in the audience and says, "I have $225." The ten-dollar bidder, if he wants the piece and is afraid of losing it might then bid $235, at which point the auctioneer would bring down his gavel in a hurry. Not too cricket, and not that common, but it happens.*

*Now, if the ten-dollar bidder is prepared to lose the piece, or doesn't care too much, he may just repeat the $210 bid and wait. The auctioneer turns to the air bidder and says, "You've changed your mind sir? Very well then, sold to the gentleman for $210." Auction-going is indeed a game for grownups!*

*There can also be air bids when absolutely no one is interested in something on the block. The auctioneer wants to prevent a "we're-not-bidding-because-you're-not-offering-anything-worthwhile" atmosphere. In addition to the obvious reason for worrying—no money coming in—he is also concerned if there are future consignors in the audience. He wants them to believe he always gets top dollar for the items he sells. So he will take air bids and try to foster competition by banging*  *the gavel and saying "sold to number X."*

127

*Unfortunately for the auctioneer, but fortunately for auction-goers, regulars at some auction houses get to know that these X numbers are "house" numbers: the numbers the auction house uses to buy back items that are not sold, either because they didn't meet the reserve, or because no one wants them.*

*I remember sitting at an auction in a little town in Missouri and watching while a really battered, poorly made, unattractive chest of drawers was "knocked down" (sold) to number twenty-one.*

*"Good lord," I said to my husband sitting beside me, "Who could have bought that? The price is ridiculous—it's not worth anything."*

*The young woman sitting in front of me turned around and said, "Oh, don't worry about that. It's sold to number twenty-one—that's the house number."*

---

about imperceptible movement of their left-hand pinky finger. I still marvel at how auctioneers manage to pick up these signals, but they do, because they pay attention to the people they know are interested.

During an auction at Christie's, New York, of French Impressionist and modern paintings (belonging, among others, to Henry Ford), I remember watching the bidding with fascination. A stunning woman in an equally stunning white Chanel suit trimmed with black braid bid for Van Gogh's *Garden of the Poet, Arles* with the slightest nod of her well-coiffed silvery blonde hair. Each nod meant she was willing to go another $50,000 or $100,000. She lost the bid to a London buyer when the price went to $5.2 million, but consoled herself with a successful bid at a mere $2.9 million for Paul Gauguin's *Beach at Pouldu.*

It was at this same auction, with the president of Christie's, David Bathurst, calling the bids, that much-too-subtle signals resulted in a real mixup. Two dealers and friendly competitors, sitting in almost a direct line

with each other, each thought he had won a Paul
Cézanne painting, *Peasant in a Blue Shirt*. When they
chatted after the auction and discovered their confusion,
they returned to the podium. Since neither would agree
to reopen the bidding, Mr. Bathurst, as was his prerogative, settled the dispute in favor of one of the dealers.

How about you? Should you be one of the eyebrow
twitchers, ear tuggers, hair patters, or wave-of-the-cigar
types? If you want to be, why not—after you've been
around a while and made your contacts with auctioneers.
But in the beginning auctioneers advise you to keep it
simple and bid with something clearly visible so you're
sure you won't be missed.

If it's an auction where numbered paddles are given to
bidders, use them, but not as fans! The number is clearly
visible, and the auction clerk can easily see who is the
winning bidder. Russell Burke of Sloan's in Washington
says a pen is usually not a good signal; so many people
are busy using them to make notes in the catalog that
they are easily missed. The important point is to use
something that is unmistakable, or (as I've said) to bid
clearly and loudly, so that you're not overlooked.

Different auction houses have different methods of
keeping track of the sales. Some have aides who come
right to your seat to record the sale; others simply keep
records and count on you to go to the appropriate place
(an office or, at an outdoor auction, a specified location)
to pick up your purchase. Either way, mixups do occur,
so you have to be wary. You should be especially alert
when the house does not use numbered cards or paddles
to be sure that the clerk recording your sales gets your
correct number.

If you are identified as the successful bidder for something when you in fact dropped out before the final bid,
or if someone else is designated the successful bidder for
an item you think is yours, don't let the mixup pass. You
will either get stuck with something you don't want or
lose out on something you do want. *Immediately,* say

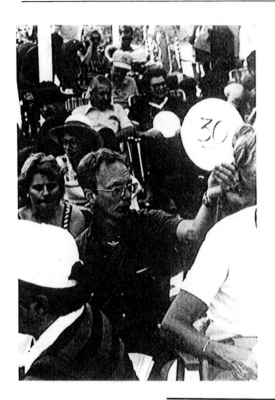 

auctioneers, raise your hand, your paddle, whatever, and say there has been a mistake. The time to correct the error is on the spot when the article can be correctly assigned, or, if need be, reauctioned.

What happens if, for a variety of reasons (you had to leave for a few moments, you were distracted by the arrival of your spouse or friends), you do miss bidding for something you really wanted? It is sometimes possible, if the successful bidder was a dealer, that you can buy the object from the dealer—at a profit to him, of course. Sometimes the auction house will act as the intermediary for you, even if the successful bidder was not a dealer. In any case, they won't reveal the name of the new owner, but they will forward your request. It's worth a try.

There will also be times when the auctioneer will say a lot has been withdrawn ("bought in," in the jargon of the trade) because the on-the-floor bid has not met the presale reserve, the minimum price at which it can be sold. When this happens you can mention to the auction house that you are interested in the article, and the house will sometimes be able to arrange for you to buy it. There's no guarantee that the auction house or cosignor of the article will be willing, but again it's worth a try.

What if you bid successfully for something, regret it, and want to take back your bid? Legally, you can't. Once you've been the successful bidder the item is yours, and you owe the auction house the full price plus whatever fees were involved. Auction houses are fully within their rights in refusing to make any adjustments—but sometimes they will bend a little. As an auctioneer said to me, "After all, we are human." They might, for instance, allow you to reconsign the item, and have them reauction it for you. (Very often it goes for less than your bid, since dealers and others realize it's been around for quite a while.) However, you would still be liable for the costs involved, which could include, in addition to what you've already paid as the buyer, anything from a seller's fee to the cost of advertising. Of course, when it's resold you get the money it brings, so you're not out of pocket for the entire amount. But obviously this is a big hassle that you don't need. So, if you're not sure you want something, it's better to pass it up.

*Picking Up Your Purchases*

Let's say you've made several successful bids. What then? Where do you pick up your purchases? How do you pay? Where do you pay? To repeat, just briefly, what we talked about in the previous chapters: You pay the full amount plus any fees with either cash, traveler's checks, a credit card, or a check. If you are using credit by means of a check, you often can't get your merchan-

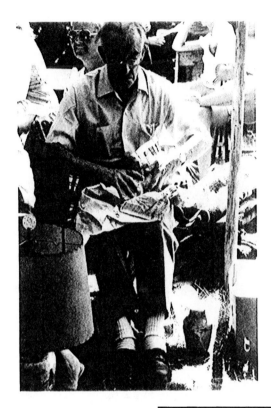 

dise until the check clears, unless you've already established your credit rating with the auction house.

Let's consider first the procedure for getting small purchases, objects you can take with you either by carrying them or by putting them in your car. At very informal country auctions one of the ring men will often simply hand you whatever you've bought, your neighbors will lean over to get a better look and congratulate you, and you can go right to the cashier, pay for it, and take it with you.

At auctions held on-site—house and estate sales—it's customary to have one area set aside where the ring men take the things as they are bought, and another area set aside with a cashier or cashiers. Usually they are near

132

the entrance to the auction area so that they can give you a number if you want to bid, and take a deposit (returnable, as noted earlier, if you don't buy). Sometimes you go and get your purchase, take it to the cashier, and then pay. More often, the process is reversed, and you pay first and then go to get your purchases.

The process is not too different at the regular auction galleries, but the timing may be different, particularly for evening auctions. Sometimes you can pick up your small purchases on the very day you buy them; other times you may have to wait until the following day. Typically, there is an office where you pay, and another area where you go to get your purchase. Some auction houses will have employees on hand to help you wrap or to supply boxes; others simply have some supplies, such as wrapping and tissue paper; at still others you are strictly on your own. To keep your life as simple as possible I just want to repeat my recommendation that you call in advance to check on the arrangements and the office hours—and that you have some supplies on hand, just in case.

The little things aren't the problem. It's the larger pieces that won't fit into your van or car that could cause difficulty. If you think you're going to need some special help with moving, again, as I mentioned earlier, these arrangements have to be made in advance, since auction houses have strict rules about when you have to pick up your purchases.

*Bidding From a Distance*

What if you've studied the catalog or have gone to the presale exhibition, and you've seen something you like—but you can't go to the auction? The good news is that you don't have to be present at an auction to bid. You can also bid by mail, telephone, or telex, as an absentee bidder.

When you see something you would like to bid on in an auction catalog or at a presale exhibition, you can ask the house to bid in your behalf. The house will bid for you as if you were there competing with other bidders, and will not exceed the upper limit you set on your bid. (An auction house will *not* accept a straight "buy" bid—the instruction to go ahead and continue the bidding regardless of the ultimate price—a restriction that is a safeguard for the house and for you.)

The process works something like this. Most catalogs have a form that authorizes the house to bid on your behalf up to the limit you set, or perhaps to the next highest multiple closest to your maximum bid, so that there is some leeway. Some auction houses have separate bid forms. In any event, the forms have a space for you to enter the lot number, the description, the bid price, your name, address, the sale number, the date, your phone number, and so on. If you don't want to use a bid form, you can send the same information by letter, telex, or cable, or you may enter the bid on the phone as long as you send a written confirmation later. (In most cases, you have to establish credit with the auction house by giving some kind of bank reference in advance.)

Absentee bidding is a regular part of the auction business, and so at most auctions an employee of the house will have a list of absentee bidders and their bids. Depending on the size of the auction house, or the number of lots in a particular sale, that employee may also be the clerk who is recording the sale, or an employee whose only job is to bid for the absentee bidders, or even someone who sits in the audience and bids anonymously for an absentee. But in any case the system is the same: The employee is your surrogate, and bids as you would bid if you were there, trying to get you the best—that is, the lowest—price.

Here are two examples of how absentee bidding works. Suppose, for instance, that you go on your lunch hour to a presale exhibition and see a brass bucket, needing a good polishing but otherwise in fine condition. You would love to have it to use as a wastebasket. (You've seen new ones, about eight inches smaller and not nearly as nice, selling for $60 and more.) You consult

the "catalog," in this case a five-page typewritten list of the items coming up for sale with their presale estimates. The brass bucket is number fifteen, meaning it will probably be sold during the first hour of the sale, which starts at 10:00 a.m.—and you can't possibly be there. The presale estimate is $20 to $40.

You complete the absentee bid form that the auction provides, and enter your top bid: $40. Then you leave the form at the office.

On the day of the auction someone opens the bid for the bucket at $10. Ms. Smith, of the auction house, bids $15 for you. Someone bids $20; someone else $25, Ms. Smith says $30, no one tops that and the bucket is yours for $30. Ms. Smith calls you, you come to the auction house the next day, pay the $30 and take the bucket home.

Or suppose you want to buy an early American rocking chair. You see an auction ad for a sale of early American furniture, send for the catalog ($5 by mail), and note a description of a chair that seems to be just what you want. The presale estimate, $200 to $300, seems

reasonable so you complete the mail-order bid, setting an upper limit of $300, and send it off. During the auction someone from the auction house bids for you, and you win the bid at $300. The auction house notifies you by mail that you are successful and asks you to send a check covering the hammer price ($300) plus a ten-percent buyer's premium, plus the cost of packing and shipping, which they arrange. When your check clears, the rocker is shipped, at your risk, by the auction house.

What I've outlined here is a general description. In just about all instances there is no charge for bidding for you. But there are variations in the way different auction houses handle their absentee bids. Some will call you; others expect you to check with them. Some will accept your mail-order bid with bank references and no deposit. Others require a deposit of ten to twenty percent, with the proviso that your money will be returned in about a month if your bid is unsuccessful. You are always responsible for the buyer's premium if that's a rule of the house, even if you're an absentee bidder. And you are also responsible for the sales tax if there is one.

Most houses either charge nothing for their service in arranging the mailing or shipping or, if there is a charge, it is usually minimal—maybe $10 to $20 or so. Just about all of them, however, will add to your bill all the actual mail, insurance, packing, and shipping charges. They are experienced and provide these services in the best way to guarantee that your purchase arrives safely and intact. (They make mistakes, of course.) There may be a time lapse of several weeks or several months between the successful bid and when you get your purchase, depending on what you've bought, how far it has to be shipped, and so on.

To make this process as easy as possible, remember that the foremost auction rule applies: everything is sold as is. However, many auction houses will, if you ask for it, send you a more complete description than the one that appears in the catalog, giving further details on condition and any repairs or restoration. You can also get more details by phone.

One universal bit of advice from the auction houses: If you are using a form, be sure to fill it out completely. Double-check on this before you mail it. If you are not using a form, it's even more important that you include all the information needed: a complete address including apartment number and office and home phone, with area codes. (Remember, if they are calling from a different part of the country, there may be time differences.) Also include bank references, the lot number or numbers if you are bidding on several items, a description of the item or items, and the number or the date of the sale, since the auction house has many sales in the course of a year.

Absentee bids are a boon to people who can't get to an auction because they are too far away, too busy, or simply unable to come at the time the auction is scheduled. But they are also a boon to the auction house. They widen the market for the house—and these days that market is getting to be not only nationwide, but also international. In addition, mail-order bids often give the house some insight into the size of the market for a particular item, which may be more than they expected. This can be a clue to the auctioneer, on the day of the sale, that he can afford to raise the bids by $25, for instance, instead of $10, or even $50 instead of $25.

Okay, you're just about set. Let's just quickly review those tricky, hard-to-answer questions. Should you be the first bidder? How do you know how much to bid? What should your upper limit be? Here are some guidelines:

Should you open the bid? Preferably not, as I mentioned earlier, since you may start it at a higher figure than the auctioneer would. Let the auctioneer set the figure, and then you have the choice of offering something less. The auctioneer also has the choice of accepting or rejecting your lower bid. If he accepts, that's fine, and if he rejects it, you can always go higher.

How do you know how much to bid? You do your homework. The presale estimate is one clue, shopping around is another, consulting price guides is still another, and all of them together are useful in getting to know the market.

What should your upper limit be? What you consider a fair price for what you want to buy. This is something you have decided on in advance, based on the homework you've done and your carefully cultivated resistance to auction fever.

As you go to auction you'll notice that auctioneers never say "Going, going, gone," which used to be part of the traditional auctions. Why not? One auctioneer says it gives people "too much time to think." Between the first and second "going" they can still change their minds and drop out. These days you're more apt to hear "All done," or "Fair warning," and a quick bang of the hammer.

Remember that an auction is a contest between auctioneer and bidder. As a bidder you want a slow pace and little competition, so prices stay low. The auctioneer wants a fast pace and much competition. The speed makes people worry that they don't have a chance unless they bid quickly, which makes the prices go up. Sometimes the bidder wins, sometimes the auctioneer—but it's always the same competitive game.

To give you fair warning on how best to play the game, go on to the next chapter, which offers some antidotes to the malady that lurks at every auction: auction fever.

# 8  AUCTION FEVER— SOME PREVENTIVE MEDICINE

Now for a moment of truth. Auctions aren't all fun and games. As you become a participant, one thing you'll observe is the skill of the auctioneer in fostering the competitive spirit underlying all auctions. Auctioneers say their favorite customers are two buyers who dislike each other, preferably intensely, and bid for something against each other just to keep the other person from having it. But animosity is rarely the source of competitive bidding. More often, it's simply a "macho" feeling: two people (women can be macho, too) proving that they can afford something as well as the next person and the hell with the money involved.

I've witnessed this rush of competitive bidding in New York City, between two rare-book dealers bidding for ancient encyclopedias—scholarly gentlemen who nodded to each other across the room before the auction started and then, from opposite corners without so much as a glance in the other's direction, bid against each other with fierce determination. And I've witnessed it outside an auction barn in Buckner, Missouri, between two farmers vying for a serviceable used wheelbarrow. They stood within a foot of each other and bid by shaking their heads slightly as the auctioneer turned first to one, then to the other.

In each case, the bidding went beyond the sensible price—the amount dealers could probably get for reselling the encyclopedia or that the farmers would have to pay for a new wheelbarrow. And in each case, the nonbuyers just sat on their hands or shifted on their feet, watching the drama with fascination, their appreciation made all the sweeter by the fact that they and their egos weren't involved—this time! It was quite obvious that both pairs of men had succumbed to that disease of auction-goers: auction fever. It's present at every auction; auctioneers know it very well and are happy to encourage it. It's good for their financial health.

What are the symptoms of auction fever? The auction-goer gets carried away by the competitive atmosphere, the excitement, the desire to be a part of the auction, the self-induced reassurance that if others are bidding, it must be something of value up there on the block—and soon prices are going up and up, sometimes way beyond the established value of what's being auctioned.

A vivid example of contagious auction fever occurred at the Los Angeles auction of part of the Garrett collection of rare coins in March 1980. More than one hundred years ago, T. Harrison Garrett, a railroad executive, began a collection of coins that ultimately was revered by all coin collectors. Accordingly, the announcement that the collection was going to be auctioned carried the title, "The Sale of the Century." When the coins were sold in Los Angeles and New York, no one was particularly surprised that record after record was broken. But there was

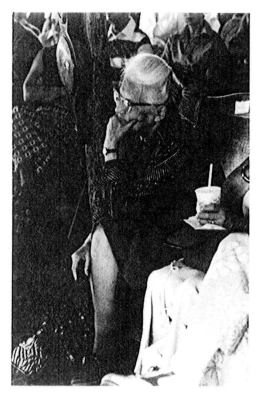

surprise that auction-goers often paid four, five, even eight times the going market price. Coin dealers and auctioneers agreed there was "no way" that collectors who bought at these inflated prices could recover their money if they tried to resell the coins, at least not in the foreseeable future. How did the experts account for these unreal prices? Sentiment, for one reason; people buying just to say they had part of the Garrett collection. But most of all, auction fever; people in the grip of a kind of "mass hysteria"—not harmful, except to the pocketbooks of the auction-goers, but slightly mad just the same.

Few auction-goers are totally immune. The head of one of the South's most prestigious auction houses, in

business for more than forty years, confesses that he, too, is still subject to auction fever. He has bid on items he really didn't want, at auctions for auctioneers, just because he was caught up in the competition.

One psychiatrist confessed to me that although he certainly knew better, he'd been bitten several times. His cure started with a successful bid for a large cabinet. It was beautiful, several other people wanted it, but he and his wife won. They were very pleased—until they got the piece home. Then they looked at each other in dismay: Where would they put it? The cabinet wasn't something they needed or even had a place for. Why did they buy it? Auction fever. Fortunately, a favorite niece had recently married and was delighted to have the cabinet as a wedding present. For a while, they were fine—and then, an-

other auction, a handsome chest, and another successful bid. This time, they had to take out a window of their house to get the chest inside. Now they think they are cured.

Dr. Lynn K. Roney, a psychologist at the University of Iowa and an auction-goer, also admits to having succumbed to auction fever on occasion. Her analysis of one of the motivations that lets people get carried away is the personal (if subconscious) feeling that "I'm not going to let that other person win over me, because if he/she wins, I've lost self-esteem." This competitive urge sometimes becomes especially strong if large sums of money are *not* involved. Then the feeling is, "I can't let him/her win if just another $10 will let *me* win." Of course, these ten-dollar bids add up, and before you know it, you can spend $50, $60, $100 more than you had planned.

*145*

*Beating Auction Fever*

What's the cure for auction fever? Preventive medicine. As Dr. Roney says, "Don't get your ego so invested in the process that you can't quit, because then, if you do quit, you think of yourself as a 'loser.' "

Standard—and good—advice. Decide *in advance* how much you are willing to pay for something you need or want. Leave yourself some flexibility, consider that you might go ten percent above this limit if you want the article very badly. *Then abide by your decision.* If you think you really can't, you might do as one veteran auction-goer does; he enjoys going to auctions, but he has no faith in his ability to stay out of the competition. So, through the mail, he submits a bid which is his absolute upper limit. Then he goes to the auction anyway, and enjoys watching the fun without risking excessive demands on his pocketbook.

Will you miss out on some things by sticking to your limit? Quite possibly, yes, Will you regret it? Quite possibly, yes. But that regret is better than getting stuck with something you really don't want, or something that isn't a bargain, especially if you have to add in the costs of taking out a window, or need to rearrange part of your home to accommodate something you bought impulsively.

You will enjoy an auction more and be a better buyer if you act more like the professionals who go, the dealers. They've done their homework, so they know values of the goods being auctioned, and they set dollar limits, because they know they have to resell at a higher price in order to earn a profit. You can afford to go higher than they can, because you are buying for yourself (which is why dealers are not at all happy about more and more customers going directly to the source, the auction, instead of buying through them). But look at it this way: Even if you go to auctions in your Mercedes-Benz or Rolls-Royce and count on your chauffeur to wrap your

packages and get them home, you don't want to get stung. That's no fun and no bargain.

Here is good advice on this whole subject from Bernard Gallo, who started in the auction business at age seven, when his auctioneer father handed him a broom in his auction house and said, "start sweeping." Mr. Gallo, now a senior vice-president with Butterfield and Butterfield in San Francisco, told me: "Learn to hear only the *bid*. Then you won't be tempted to indulge in competition with someone you know and don't like, or someone you take an instant dislike to, or just because you are suddenly bitten by the competitive bug."

"But what if you lose a chance to get something you want?" I asked him.

"One very important thing all auction-goers must remember," he replied, "is that there's always another auction. If you've lost out on something you want, you can probably get something similar another time—

*147*

maybe even something better. When bidding," he went on, "and you've settled on a price, try not to think about how far you've come, or that you drove the last thirty miles in the heat because the air-conditioning in your car broke down, or how long you've waited until the object you're interested in finally comes on the block. If you think about these things, you tend to forget the price you decided on and give in to uncontrolled impulse."

"How about buying things simply with the idea of re-selling them?"

"A bad idea. The purpose of buying is not as an investment, but to enjoy something and have it better your life. You should bid for something after you consider its quality, its rarity and its age—although something old is not *necessarily* good. Old junk is still junk. Your criterion should be not the dollar price that you paid, but that you bought something that contributes to your happiness."

# 9   WHAT INFLUENCES PRICES— PAST, PRESENT, AND FUTURE

The auction fantasy of many of us is to buy something, or even better several things, for a low price, that will in the future become super-popular *and* high-priced. Ideally, our purchase would be a collection that would be delightful and useful both to have and to hold. The collection would also be large enough so that at the proper (read profitable) time we could keep the best pieces for continued pleasure and conversation, while the next-best pieces would go off to the auction market to be sold at record-breaking prices. We can dream, can't we? But the serious question is, can we do more than dream? Do we have a chance at making our dream a reality?

Part of the answer is price, so let's take a look at prices at auction and see what affects them. Until time machines are perfected outside the pages of science fiction, it's impossible to predict future prices with any kind of certainty. But it is possible to identify some key factors. Briefly, prices are affected by major currents in the world of politics, economics, and technology; by geography; by changing social attitudes and values; and, on a much less cosmic scale, by crazes, fads, and foibles. Plus (and it's a big plus) publicity, promotion, and hoopla.

As we examine how some of these factors affected auction prices in the past, we'll get some clues as to what might happen in the future. This is by no means an exhaustive survey, but at least you'll get an idea as to why prices behave the way they do, which is, sometimes, neither predictably nor rationally.

When we speak of prices being affected by such elements as politics, crazes, and publicity, we are talking about the "current market price." In the auction field this is loosely defined as the average price of an object sold within the past year, as determined by the records kept by major auction houses around the country and compiled and then published by various newspapers, magazines, and books. Obviously, since the market is continuous, since it's impossible to make exact comparisons because so many items are one- or few-of-a-kind, and since there is always a time gap between when the prices are received and when they are published, reports on "current market price" cannot be anything more than the most general of guidelines. Nevertheless, the reports are useful, since they are consulted by the people who make up the marketplace: the auctioneers, dealers, collectors, and the auction-goers.

*The Changing Market Price*

Now let's consider some variables affecting current market prices.

• *Regional differences.* Prices are often significantly affected by regional differences in taste. And such regional differences in taste often mean regional differences in price. As a buyer of, say, colonial furniture, you might get a better buy traveling out of your immediate area, or taking a chance on bidding by mail, even with the additional packing and shipping costs. On this last point, two dealer-auctioneers I know, one from the state of Washington and the other from across the country in New Hampshire, have told me that the best buys in oak furniture are in the Middle West. It pays them to buy there, despite the cost of shipping, because they can get higher prices back home, on either coast, whether they sell directly to a customer or through their auctions.

Other examples: Victorian and Nineteenth-century English and French furniture sells well in the South, partly because oil-rich southerners have money to spend and currently are choosing to spend it on restoring old houses, and partly because these old houses provide the high ceilings and spacious rooms that set off such furniture.

The New England area, on the other hand, is well known for preserving its heritage of colonial and early American furniture, which is constantly being auctioned off to thousands of summer visitors. In contrast, nearby New York is known for buyers who will pay high prices for more elaborate pieces (or, at the moment, trendy art nouveau and art deco pieces), which means bargain prices for buyers of "country" furniture.

Los Angeles is a different market altogether and can be totally unpredictable. Not surprisingly for people who live in movieland, Angelenos are visually oriented, and they are attracted to and will pay high prices for goods with strong, perhaps even flashy, eye appeal. Unlike San Franciscans, who are eager to preserve an older tradition, these southern Californians have a different, more recent tradition of collecting and furnishing their homes. Because they live in a hotter, drier climate and have a more casual lifestyle, they turn to more casual furniture styles. Pieces from Eighteenth-century America aren't their style.

*151*

• *Changing tastes.* If you were to look at charts showing the rise, fall, and sometimes rise again of, for instance, American furniture styles, you'd think you were looking at charts of the stock market or the Consumer Price Index. No matter if it's Queen Anne, Chippendale, Federal, Empire, Victorian, or Golden Oak, they all have had their peaks and valleys, though some are less erratic than others. Nor is there any basic reason for the rise or the fall. Who can say, logically, why people loved Federal-style furniture in the twenties, ignored it or maybe even gave it to charity in the fifties, and are now busy buying it back in the eighties? There is no underlying logic. People's tastes change, and prices, like Mary's little lamb, are sure to follow.

I find it hard to believe that Russel Wright dishes are, to quote *Business Week,* a "hot collectible." In New

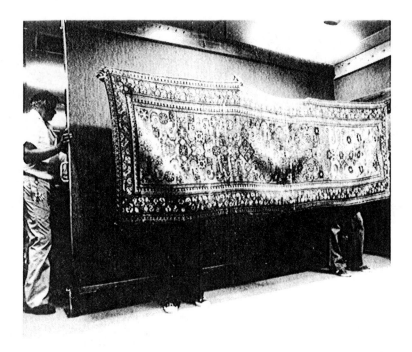

York, a set of eight dinner plates in the preferred shades of chartreuse or green sold for $800 in the spring of 1980; however, in the Midwest, where those colors were not at all the favorites, you could buy a set for about $50. I distinctly remember shedding not a tear as my complete set of chartreuse Russel Wright service for four slowly broke or chipped during the early years of my marriage, until finally I just got rid of them. Since my sisters had given me the dishes, I kept the sugar bowl—no top—and the cream pitcher. Both now have plants growing out of them.

• *Social conditions.* The civil-rights movement in the United States led to a tremendous interest in black history, going all the way back to the African ancestors of American blacks. One observer of the auction and art scene noted that forty years ago you couldn't give away examples of native African art—masks, statuettes, and

*153*

carvings of tribal gods from Liberia, the Ivory Coast, Gabon, and elsewhere. These are now selling to collectors and museums for thousands and even hundreds of thousands of dollars. This same kind of ethnic interest, also emerging from the civil-rights movement, spread to the American Indian, which in turn led to an interest in and a demand for the art works and crafts of the American Indians. Needless to say, prices of Indian artifacts increased.

• *Politics.* A revolution in a country, not surprisingly, affects prices. The Iranian rug was one good example, but perhaps not the way you might anticipate. Wouldn't you have guessed that the revolution would have driven prices up immediately? Surprisingly, the reverse was true. Many Iranians came to this country, and since they lacked cash, they put some of their rugs on the market. Increased supply, no increase in the demand: lower prices. The Portuguese revolution offered another surprising example. Wealthy Portuguese, who had previously been in the market for many collector's items, suddenly found themselves without accessible funds. The Portuguese had been buyers of fine porcelain. When they stopped buying after the revolution, their withdrawal affected the market for porcelain, and the prices of porcelain dropped.

• *Competition.* Sometimes competition comes from utterly unexpected and certainly unpredictable sources. Take baseball cards. Baseball cards have been a collectible fad for a long time, starting with the little boys who swapped them in the school play yard. But then when the little boys grew up, they, and lots of other people, went on collecting the cards, and the result was some very high prices. A Mickey Mantle baseball card, for instance, sold for about $500 in 1978–79; only a year later it was selling for $2,500. (If you've tossed these cards away or made your little boy toss them away, time out while you kick yourself. And if you think you feel badly, think how Mickey Mantle must feel if he doesn't have any!)

But there is another angle to this. Top prices attract competition. The Tops Chewing Gum Company, which had a monopoly on baseball players picture cards, recently had the monopoly ended, and Fleer Corporation of Philadelphia was allowed to move into the business. Nobody knows what's going to happen when Fleer obtains its license, supposedly sometime in 1981. But depending on the kinds of cards they produce, the activity is probably going to affect the price of the baseball cards, making some people's collections more valuable, some people's

less valuable. So you see that luck and chance can always intervene; prices are not forever.

• *Individuals.* Silver in 1979–80 is a good example. Thanks to the attemps by the Hunt brothers to become the world's largest owners of silver bullion (they denied reports that they were trying to corner the silver market), the price of silver bullion went from about $6 an ounce to almost $50 an ounce. All the media stories about the Hunts and their maneuvers led people who had forgotten about Uncle George's silver-handled hairbrushes to pull them out of the bottom of the closet, and to dig out the old silver baby spoons that had been lying around in drawers, the jewelry no one wore, the coffee sets used only at Christmas. Many antiques someone might have loved to have owned were melted down just for the value of the bullion. And it was a self-feeding process: the more publicity, the more attics searched and the more silver pieces melted down.

But when the price of silver bullion plummeted from about $50 to $11 an ounce (as a result of government intervention), did antique silver fall at the same rate? Or as precipitously? Again the answer might surprise you: No. For one thing, there is a time lag, from weeks to months, in the pricing of silver goods at auctions (and at retail stores). But more significantly, to quote from a report in the May 1980 issue of *Art and Auction:* "Many examples of highly worked silver are increasingly sought after—apparently the publicity surrounding the big 'February meltdown' increased fears that good examples of nineteenth and twentieth century workmanship had been scrapped forever."

• *Reserves.* I've mentioned this before, but no discussion of price is complete without talking about reserves. You'll remember that a reserve is the confidential minimum price acceptable to the owner of an item; if the bidding does not reach this minimum, the item is not sold but is "bought in," that is, taken off the block and disposed of in some other way. It may be returned to its owner, which can be the auction house, put aside to be sold at a different sale, or sold to a dealer. In order to protect the consignor, no matter who it is, auctioneers have the right to take part in the bidding, customarily state this right in their catalogs, and do indeed have employees in the audience bidding for individual items.

### Prices and the Professionals

This brings us to the way some auctioneering professionals affect prices.

Take auctioneers for example. Their primary job is to

*157*

get the maximum price on the goods they sell. How? Through their skill at creating excitement and keeping an audience interested; by maintaining a pace that's fast enough to convince people they have to get in on the bid quickly or they'll lose out, but not so fast that potential bidders are missed; and, very importantly, by knowing enough about the merchandise to tout its virtues and start the bid at a reasonable level. If an auctioneer starts too low, the article might not reach its potential. But if it's too high, no one will bid, he'll have to start at a lower figure, and the audience may still just stare at the ceiling, the walls, and their neighbors until he lowers his bid even further.

When veteran auctioneers are training newcomers, they remind them that anyone can step up to the podium and sell, but the good auctioneer is the one who can get the most money at a sale. To quote from a training manual: "Your success depends upon inducing your buyers to pay more than they at first seemed willing to pay. Anyone can usually get what the buyers have made up their mind they are willing to pay, but the auctioneer who can

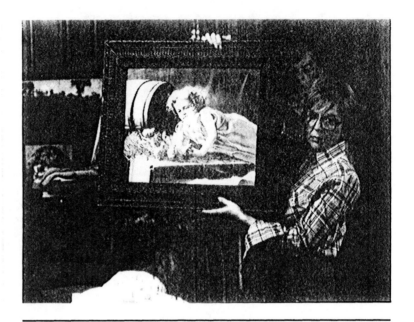

influence and induce them into paying an extra five or ten percent is the one who will get the business."

Since dealers make up a good part of any auction audience, they too have a big influence on prices. All auction-goers wonder at some point about bidding against dealers and also about competing with dealer "rings."

Let's consider the dealer first. As I've mentioned, he is understandably not too happy about the current boom in auctions. People who used to come to him to buy, partly because they relied on his expertise and partly because he had on hand the items they wanted, now are bypassing him, acquiring their own expertise, and buying for themselves at auctions.

Does this mean that the dealers sitting near you are your antagonists? Not necessarily. They help keep the auction market going, since they comprise anywhere from forty to sixty percent of the market, depending on what's sold. (For some items, such as jewelry, they are often about ninety percent of the market.) They also can

*159*

## Some Sources for Auction Prices

*If you are interested in checking prices of art and antiques sold at auction, one guide is the* Art & Antique Auction Review. *It's a thirty-two-page monthly bulletin that gets its prices from major auction houses, and tries to cover the categories of collectibles most interesting to people in this country—including furniture, glass, porcelains, American coins, American silver and pewter—and to report on items in the medium price ranges, from about $100 and up. A subscription costs $36 for twelve issues plus postage and handling. They will send you a free trial copy. Write to* Art & Antique Auction Review, c/o University Arts, Inc., IFM Building, Old Saybrook, CT 06475.

*The thirteenth edition of* The Kovels' Antiques Price List *is a report of the actual sale prices of antiques sold in the United States between June 1979 and June 1980. A few of the prices are from auctions, say the authors, Ralph and Terry Kovel, but "most are from shops and shows." The book excludes prices of fine art paintings, books, comic books, stamps, coins and a few other categories, all of which are covered in specialized books. The book is interestingly illustrated with both color and black and white photographs, and is well-organized. (Crown Publishers, Inc., paperback, $9.95.)*

*The* Official Sotheby Park Bernet Price Guide to Antiques & Decorative Arts *lists the final sale price of 33,-000 items auctioned off at Sotheby's during the 1978-1979 auction season. The book covers 24 major collecting areas, including old masters, contemporary paintings, folk art, and Americana. It has 1300 black and white photographs, brief essays on the market for various categories of items, and a useful explanation about the different degrees of certainty that are possible in establishing the authenticity of an object. The table of contents is extensive, making it comparatively easy to locate particular objects. (Simon and Schuster, paperback, $9.95; hardcover, $22.50.)*

reinforce your impressions of value, since, for the most part, they *are* knowledgeable. Further, they are sometimes an aid in keeping prices down, since they won't raise a bid more than is necessary to stay in the game. (They usually stay within preset limits, based on what they think the piece is worth, considering their overhead and the profit they would like to earn.) So, if you come to recognize the dealers at an auction (and you will after a while), and you buy something one or two bids higher than the price at which the dealers dropped out, you can legitimately feel that you have gotten a good buy.

But how about dealers' rings? These are also known as dealers' pools: dealers join together in advance, agree not to bid against each other in order to keep prices low, and then have a second auction among themselves. The dollar difference between the successful bid price at the auction and the price at the private auction is then shared among the dealers under a formula they've agreed upon. Here is some background on dealers' rings that I think will help set your mind at rest.

*161*

Are there dealers' rings? Would any dealer admit to this for the record? Of course not. Off the record, dealers and auctioneers told me yes. Are they permanent, fixed institutions? Not at all. They are, according to my sources, loose confederations that form, break up, form again, depending on what they're interested in and for how long. The ring can have three members, or five or seven or more. There are rings at country auctions as well as at big-city auctions. Occasionally some (not all) auctioneers will act in collusion with rings, for a variety of reasons from returning favors to accepting bribes.

How do rings affect prices for the private auction-goer? If the ring is bidding to keep prices low, and the bidding is open and you want something very badly, you can beat them simply by being willing to bid until you get what you want. The dealers may not like you, but that's their problem.

You may have a problem, however, if you are selling something at an auction, because the ring can prevent your antique dining-room set, for instance, from getting a fair price. Your only protection against this happening is a reserve, so that it cannot be sold at less than the reserve.

But you needn't be unduly worried about all this. There are strong factors that work against rings. It is part of the responsibility of a reputable auction house to guard against the rings, by being sure that all bidders are recognized and have a chance to bid. It's also true that, as the auction market expands, it becomes more difficult for rings to operate. More and more catalogs are crisscrossing the country these days, enabling everyone to bid on any items their hearts desire and their checkbooks allow. And people themselves are crisscrossing not only the country but the world, to drop in on auctions in New York, New Orleans, San Francisco, or Chicago, to bid and to buy. The larger the market in numbers and in geography, the more difficult it becomes for rings to operate. A skillfull auctioneer, a determined dealer repre-

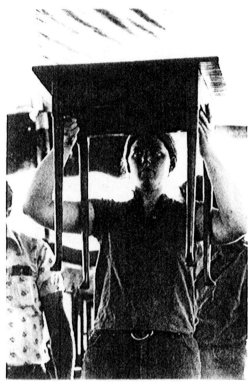

senting a very rich client, a collector who has been smitten by auction fever—all are more likely to give you unwelcome competition than is a dealer's ring.

What all of us want, when we buy at auction, is to know that we have paid a price that is "fair" (although admittedly a fair price can be difficult to define, since so often an object's price is a unique composite of opinion, history, condition, and rarity). In general, however, the consensus on a "fair" price at auction is that it is somewhere below retail and above wholesale. Sometimes you will be clever, or shrewd, or lucky, or all three, and get a terrific bargain—and it really does happen. But, quite objectively, you can say you got a fair price if you paid less than you would have paid to a dealer.

*163*

*Buy Now, Cash in Later?*

Okay—now we've looked at many factors that influence prices. How likely is it that you could realistically anticipate soaring jumps in value? And behind this question is the more basic one: Is buying at auction an investment strategy you should consider?

Certainly, one of the big selling points for going to auctions, constantly pushed by auction houses in their ads and fed by media stories about record-breaking prices, is the potential for profit. There are quotes from brokers, bankers, and auction vice-presidents that antiques and collectibles have been a major way not just to keep up with inflation but also to beat it. Both these facts are true, but—and it's a big but—some facts are more true than others.

Yes, it's true that antiques have held their value more than other forms of investments. *Some* antiques, not all. Just about everyone I've spoken to in the auction and antique business says the same thing: *Quality holds its price,* almost irrespective of what happens to the rest of the market. And you don't need a degree in economics to know the reason why: Quality is expensive.

But here's the essence of the problem: People who can afford quality (usually a very small percentage of the buying public) are different from you and me. Not only are they richer, their riches are not affected very much by what happens to the economy. Auction houses may run ads saying, "You don't have to be a millionaire to buy at auction," which is definitely true or else I wouldn't have written this book. But it doesn't hurt to be a millionaire if you want to buy the masterpiece paintings, the sterling-silver tea sets used by royalty, the exquisitely carved and decorated furniture in superb condition. These are the rare antique items that truly have increased in value in the past decade and have outpaced inflation. And these are the items you and I and our friends will not be bidding for at auctions.

The truth is that not all antiques are like money in the

bank. Susan Seliger, antiques columnist for the *Washington Star,* put it this way: "Not everything called an antique really is an antique, and even in a democracy not all antiques were created equal. Some pieces only get older, not better."

Much the same argument can be made against presumably inflation-proof collectibles. There is no guarantee that collectibles—which rarely have intrinsic value, but are simply part of a fad—won't fade from glory faster than they achieved that glory. "Yesterday's throwaways will also be tomorrow's throwaways."

The point I'm making is simply this. Just as you have to be very clear about your upper limit before you decide to bid on something so you won't be carried away, you also have to be very clear about your *objectives* when you buy at an auction. Are you buying primarily for investment? If so, you have to accept some of the special characteristics of the art, antique, and collectibles market. It is, in the jargon of the investment world, "illiquid," that is, you can't count on getting a return on your investment quickly without the possibility of cash loss. Because you're dealing with a very specialized market, you can have very special problems.

Antiques and art collectibles are not necessities, so in times of recession no one can predict what will happen to their value. In past recessions some goods have advanced, some have kept their value, and some have fallen drastically. Even in ordinary times, no one can foretell what will happen to individual prices of individual items. As an example, let's consider paintings. If you have bought Renoirs, Van Goghs or Picassos at an auction, you aren't going to be too concerned with the way recessions could affect their prices. On the other hand, if you have bought modern surrealist paintings, or the paintings of soup cans and ketchup bottles that were popular in the seventies, you might be worried. Who can say if their value will stay the same, advance, or decline?

The following guidelines summarize the consensus of

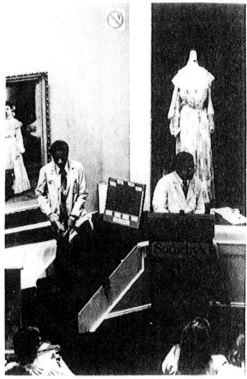

professional investment counselors, experts at auction houses, and dealers in art and antiques on how to buy as an investment.

1. Buy quality—the classics, the one- or few-of-a-kind; the pieces of furniture or decorative objects or accessories that have an intrinsic value simply because they are so well made or so beautiful that they are almost immune to changing tastes.

2. Be prepared to wait a long time for a return. Ten to fifteen years is probably the best advice, though some items might appreciate in value before that time.

3. Be wary of the glossy promotional pieces that can fill your mailboxes, promising, often very subtly, that a certain kind of art, antique, photograph, or collectible is

*166*

guaranteed to go up in value. No one can really guarantee the future, unless they promise you in writing that (1) they will buy the item back from you at a given rate of appreciation and (2) they will be in business, with funds on hand, to back up that guarantee.

If you can follow these guidelines, then you can buy at auctions as an investment. If not, then you'll buy there for the many other reasons we've already discussed.

Of course, there's always the possibility that you'll hit the jackpot, and your lucky find at an auction will turn out to be a rare treasure, a signed masterpiece, the last piece missing from a collection that two millionaires who loathe each other will bid for when you decide to sell it. . . .

To paraphrase the poet Robert Browning, "Man's reach should exceed his grasp, or what's an auction for?"

# 10 YOU LOVE IT— BUT IS IT FOR REAL?

You saw it at the exhibition, and something in you said, "That's it." You checked the dimensions, and they were exactly right. You looked at the object of your dreams carefully, and saw that it was in excellent condition. Then you made the winning bid, staying within your price range. Now you're standing in line, ready to pay. But instead of being elated you're feeling a little depressed. Is it really a nineteenth-century pitcher, or an imitation from a later time? Is it an authentic Belter chair? Is it truly a Spanish painting? What's the significance of the fact that it's signed on the lower right-hand corner, but you can't make out the signature? You're beginning to have your doubts about what you bought, and about your own judgment in buying it.

Is it for real? Is it beautiful? Is it a genuine antique?

Or have you been fooled? These doubts assail everyone who buys at auction, including, sometimes, even dealers themselves. And with some justification, considering that fakes and reproductions are not unknown in the art, antique, and furniture world. Who can *swear* that a painting was painted by artist X, or a chair was built by master cabinetmaker Y, unless the person swearing was there at the time of creation? And, quite literally with antiques, that's just not possible—nor is it completely assured even with things created within our lifetime. There is always an element of doubt, since you must trust the word and reports of others.

So let's take a look at this shadowy world of is-it-or-isn't-it, and who-knows-for-sure. And then, before we're through, let's consider the possible heretical question: For auction-goers like you and me, how much and under

*169*

what circumstances does it really matter? (Fortunately, burning at the stake is no longer practiced on heretics!)

*Fakes, Copies, Reproductions, and the Rest*

Let's face it. Just about the entire field of furniture, paintings, decorative arts, silver, jewelry—all the articles that cross the auction block—can be reproduced. What's more, as auctioneers, dealers, and museum personnel will acknowledge, the field is indeed full of reproductions, imitations, and false claims, sometimes due to chicanery but just as often due to a genuine lack of knowledge and the impossibility of giving one-hundred-percent guarantees.

So if you are worried, you might draw consolation from knowing that you are not alone. Let me give you an example from the highly specialized field of rare coins, where auctions are continually setting new records. Here's what staid *Business Week* magazine had to say about this area of collecting: "The rare coin market is a garden of chicanery. Counterfeiting has always been a problem of course. In fact some marvelous fakes of ancient Greek coins, produced by a nineteenth-century German goldsmith, are so well-known that they have developed a market all their own." It isn't just old coins that are faked. "During the last decade, a steady trickle of U.S. gold coins has made its way from Europe and more and more unwary collectors are getting stung. All denominations, from $20 gold pieces down to $2.50 quarter eagles are counterfeited in Europe."

Our European cousins, as you see, still think that we are the colonials and can easily be fooled, and perhaps in some ways they are right. But it's also possible that there are Americans busy counterfeiting European coins to sell to European coin collectors!

How about the furniture field? Who can answer, authoritatively, that worrisome question: Is it an authentic antique? The very word "authentic" is treated most gingerly by those who handle antiques daily, namely the auction houses. All of them have warnings to purchasers that the customary right to return an item not properly identified in the catalog does not (in the words of one house) "extend to works executed before 1870 unless these works are determined to be counterfeit, as this is a matter of current scholarly opinion which can change a lot."

Even "antique" doesn't have a simple, clear meaning. "The term antique indicates that in our opinion the item is more than 100 years old. The term semi-antique indicates that in our opinion the item is more than fifty years old, but less than 100 years old." As you can see, age and authenticity are not easily or precisely defined.

If you think ours is an immoral age, you may be relieved to know that the temptation to substitute the reproduction for the real thing has apparently been around a long time. There is an ancient Egyptian papyrus in a museum in Stockholm, Sweden, which is a how-to-do-it manual for fabricating imitation precious gems from colored glass. (Imagine scholars working for years to decipher that papyrus, thinking that perhaps they would discover the long-lost secret of how the Egyptians preserved their mummies. Finally they find the key to the dead language, start translating—and come up with how to make fakes!)

But in all fairness, the definition of what is a copy or a counterfeit has itself been open to question, depending on the era being discussed. During the Renaissance, copying paintings was a recommended way of teaching the craft to apprentices and students. Furthermore, it was perfectly acceptable for a patron to commission an established painter to copy the work of somebody else. One of the Medicis, Ottavano, had Andrea del Sarto copy a Raphael portrait of Pope Leo X. The portrait was one of Ottavano's favorites. When he wanted to give it to a fellow nobleman, he just couldn't bear to part with it. So he

had it duplicated, and gave the copy to the nobleman as the original, without depriving himself.

Raphael himself was not above engaging in a little bit of chicanery. He painted his *Wedding of the Madonna* so much like the *Wedding of the Virgin* by his teacher, Perugino, that someone looking at them casually would consider the paintings almost identical. About half a century later, Rudolph II, the Holy Roman Emperor, ordered two court painters to make copies of the finest pictures in Venice and Rome so that he could have masterpieces in his collection in Prague. Unfortunately for art historians, the originals have never been completely sorted out from the copies.

172

When Michelangelo was a young teenager, about the time Raphael was born, and was working as an apprentice in the Florence studio of Ghirlandaio, he was assigned to copy the head of an unknown master for a Ghirlandaio customer. Michaelangelo liked the painting so much that he managed to duplicate it exactly, partly by smoking his copy to make it look good. He kept the original; the duplicate was sold to the customer. When a fellow apprentice exposed Michaelangelo's duplicity, the owner demanded to have his original returned. But even Ghirlandaio himself couldn't tell which was which.

Needless to say, there are jokes that play upon the theme of originals and forgeries, and like many aspects of humor, they reflect the truth. For instance, one of the sayings in the art trade is that Camille Corot, the nineteenth-century French Barbizon school artist, painted 2,000 pictures—and 3,000 of them are in the United States. Another saying is that at least 10,000 of Rembrandt's 700 canvases are in the United States. Nor are the jokes confined to this country. The Hotel Drouot, which is the leading Paris auction house, is rumored to have at least one fake Utrillo auctioned off every week.

One problem that makes it so difficult to uncover fakes is a consequence of the publicity given well-known collectors as they acquire their masterpieces. They are pictured on the society pages—happy faces and champagne glasses at the pre-auction parties, and sometimes again when they denote these masterpieces to museums. After getting your picture in the papers as a philanthropist or patron of the arts, who wants it known that you've been conned? One patron who did get ripped off was the former automobile magnate, Walter Chrysler, back in 1961. He had bought some of his collection from the Hartert Galleries, then in New York City, and exhibited them in Provincetown, Massachusetts, until they were identified as frauds with the help of the Arts Dealers Association. Mr. Chrysler quietly disposed of the paintings, and the Hartert Gallery closed.

But the story doesn't end there. Until very recently, there was virtually no prosecution of art forgers, and so Mr. Hartert took the remainder of his collection and stored it in a warehouse in Peekskill, New York. In the past year or two, some paintings from this warehouse "collection" have reappeared in the art world, after being sold to gullible collectors. The Federal Bureau of Investigation has become involved in some cases of suspected fraud, and, according to an article in *Art and Auction*, there are possibilities of criminal indictments not only against Hartert but also against one auction gallery. Despite this, Bonnie Burnham, executive director of the International Foundation for Art Research, a nonprofit organization that has an authentication service, says, "One wonders how many [buyers of forgeries] will come forward with evidence, and how many will, like Walter Chrysler, choose to remain silent and bury their mistakes."

Of course, not only paintings are faked. Consider the Phipps collection of eighteenth-century antiques in the Frick Collection in New York, in what used to be the Frick mansion. Two years ago, a console supposedly made by one Jean-Henri Riesener, cabinetmaker to the eighteenth-century French king Louis XVI, was discovered to be a late nineteenth-century copy. More recently, evidence suggests that two commodes are reproductions, and not originals by André-Charles Boulle, cabinetmaker to Louis XIV, the so-called Sun King. The Frick has issued a *Guide to the Galleries* that will tell visitors which is the real piece and which the reproduction—at least until further doubts arise!

Fakery extends even to specialized areas of collecting. For instance, auctioneers were warned in one issue of their trade magazine that fake scrimshaw was flooding both the American and the British markets. (Scrimshaw is whale or walrus bones or tusks that have been carved or engraved, originally by whalers in their leisure time.) The warning states: "Unlike authorized museum repro-

ductions of genuine scrimshaw items, these elaborate examples bear no mark identifying them as modern, nor do they indicate the manufacturer. The high quality of the molding and engraving in these particular pieces is causing some people to mistake them for real scrimshaw." (Considering this problem from a somewhat different viewpoint, if the quality of this scrimshaw is so excellent, can buying and owning it be so bad, *if* the price is right? And *if* it is not sold under false pretenses. Those are two big ifs, of course, and we'll get to them very shortly.)

The scrimshaw case leads to another issue that often plagues auction-goers: Is it really art? This question most often comes up when acquaintances, friends, and relatives view one of your auction buys, especially something that's a little bit, at least in their terms, unconventional—perhaps a painting or piece of sculpture by an

175

## French Forgeries With Savoir Faire

*If you have a taste for villains, you have to admire, if unwillingly, some of the art forgers. Consider Jean Charles Millet, the grandson of another famous French Barbizon school artist, Jean François Millet, who was caught selling forged paintings he said were the works of his grandfather. Jean Charles began his career by forging his ancestor's signature to paintings that had been done by students of his grandfather. He was so successful that he set up shop as a dealer in Millet paintings, with a housepainter named Cazot as a partner. Their business flourished, and Cazot then began to dabble in painting fresh canvases, first in the manner of Millet, then of Corot, Monet, and several other French painters. One reason Jean Charles Millet was able to carry out his sale of forgeries so successfully was the generous nature of at least one of "his" artists, Camille Corot, who had been eminently successful. Monsieur Corot, when he sympathized with an artist friend who was not doing well, would sign Corot to his friend's painting, which would help it sell.*

*The Jean Charles/Cazot paintings went to dealers for as much as $10,000, and were then sold for as much as $60,000. One British museum, in fact, paid over $97,000 for an "original" Millet which Jean Charles later boasted was a fake. He went on to prove that it was fake to the very experts who had certified that it was indeed an original. He and his colleagues in his company received very short sentences, since French law did not consider it a serious crime to sell forgeries to foreigners.*

unknown artist, ancient or modern. It's a question that can absolutely crush you, as your friends raise their elbows and look dubious. And it's a question that doesn't have an easy answer.

But suppose that, back in the 1870s, you had been a wealthy but eccentric Parisian or Parisienne who liked to go "slumming" at exhibitions of those "crazy" painters so scorned by the experts at the French Academy. Those "lunatic" Impressionists: Renoir, Degas, Cézanne, Sisley, Pissarro, and Monet. One of your fellow Parisians even quoted to you a review about one of the exhibitions, calling it a "grisly spectacle." A reporter had coined the term "Impressionists" from Manet's painting *Impression, soleil levant* (*Impression of the Sunrise*), and it was adopted by the critics as a term of ridicule. You told your fellow Parisian that "you didn't know what was 'art' but you knew what you liked"—and ignoring everyone's advice and their opinion that you were as crazy as those painters, you bought some of the Impressionist paintings.

Think how your heirs would have adored you, as they kept the best paintings and sold the others at auction for millions of not-so-crazy dollars! What better proof that in art, as in any other creative field, there are changing tastes. Very often, what is "art" can be determined only by the passage of time. And even then, there are ebbs and flows of popularity.

So if you don't have the millions with which to buy the recognized masterpieces, but you get something at an auction that will enhance your personal art of living, who is to say that you are not your own best critic? Your taste and your judgment could be as good as or better than that of the art critics of the past, who have often been proven totally and completely wrong.

*Does It Matter?*

In a sense, the question of what is art is similar to the issue of genuine versus fake. There used to be and perhaps still is a certain amount of snobbery toward buying anything at auctions, especially furniture. With an occasional sniff, some people would say it's really not an antique but just "used" or "secondhand" furniture. Yet who can draw the precise line between what is an antique and what is "used" or "secondhand"? There are

177

many fine pieces of furniture sold at auction houses today that are reproductions of earlier periods. They are good buys because they are far better made than much of the furniture now being produced, have intrinsic value because they are beautiful (reproductions or not), and—best of all—the price compares more than favorably with new furniture. In fact, in the resale market they might be worth as much as new furniture, though they cost less now.

At an auction, the important thing to keep in mind is that the item you are bidding for is, or should be, correctly cataloged or identified by the auction house, so that you're not being asked to pay a high "original" price for what is either an imitation or a reproduction. On this there can be no compromise. Confidence in these questions depends partly on the honesty of the auction house and partly—since they are sometimes fooled themselves—on your own knowledge and expertise.

Take heart. There are no absolutes in the art and auction world, any more than there are in real life. After you

178

have taken due care to protect your own interests, you are the only expert who can answer the important questions. Will you get a genuine gratification from your purchase? Will it fill a real need in your life—physical, emotional, even nonsensical? (I confess that I love the little mechanical bug-eyed space man I bought at an auction, and get real pleasure every time I look at him perched on top of the television.) Did you pay what you considered a reasonable price? Do you like it even if you don't know if it's art?

If your answer to such questions is yes, settle back and enjoy.

# 11  HAVE YOU THOUGHT ABOUT INSURANCE?

You've made your lucky find: the chest you've been looking for; the set of sterling you always wanted; a peacock-pattern vase to add to your collection of carnival glass; a truly lovely antique gold locket. Terrific! Now, alas, some new problems. Since what you've bought at auction adds to your worldly goods as well as your worldly pleasure, it's time to check your insurance. Brace yourself for some gloom-and-doom talk—not fun, but sensible and necessary.

To begin with, I probably don't need to tell you that burglary is on the rise, especially for gold, silver and jewelry. Educated criminals follow the auction news and may be very interested in the fact that you just bought some item of real value. Add to this the possibility of fire, storm damage, flooding, even volcanoes! And don't forget ordinary human error and carelessness; things get lost as well as stolen. It all adds up to the fact that you need insurance protection.

Your first priority is to check your current homeowner's policy. (The best time to read it is in the morning, or whenever you're freshest, because most policies are guaranteed to put you to sleep.) If you don't have a homeowner's policy because you are living in an apartment and think you can't get one, this is not so. Such insurance is increasingly available for apartment dwellers.

One problem with the typical homeowner's insurance policy is that it has a very low limit on "unscheduled property," which means anything that is *not* listed on a separate schedule. This anything would probably include the items you buy at auction, particularly china, silver, jewelry, works of art, collections of coins, stamps, and the like. In major urban areas, the policy's limit on unscheduled property could be as little as $250, and is probably not more than $500, particularly if the policy was written in the mid-1970s. Some older policies did cover silverware, but even then the top coverage was $1,000.

Homeowner's policies often have another drawback when it comes to works of art, jewelry, silver, and so on. They usually have a deductible, which makes for a good buy for property insurance but not for valuables' insurance. Let's say your policy has a $200 deductible, which means you will cover the first $200 of any loss or damage; the insurance company will cover losses of more than $200 and will charge you a lower premium than if you didn't have the deductible. (The theory is that you pay for the smaller losses in order to be able to get a better buy in coverage for the larger losses.)

But let's see how such a deductible applies to your valuables. Let's imagine that one night, while cleaning up at 2:00 a.m. after a wonderful but exhausting dinner party, you accidentally throw out one of the sterling silver spoons you recently acquired at an auction. The spoon is worth $100. Under the terms of your homeowner's $200 deductible, you couldn't collect. Obviously, you need better protection for your valuables than the protection you get from the typical homeowner's policy.

*Protecting Your Purchases*

What you need is additional coverage in the form of a *personal articles floater.* It can be written as an extension of your present homeowner or apartment dweller insurance, but it's a separate legal contract that does not duplicate the coverage you already have. A floater policy can list all items of value on an individual basis: that old camera that you found at an auction, your stamp collection, maybe an antique musical instrument, pieces of jewelry, or sterling-silver flatware.

How much protection should you have? The Insurance Information Institute recommends floater coverage if you own anything that would cost more than $500 to replace. Of course, when we're talking about antiques, the policy would have to cover items that probably cannot be literally replaced—but you still want to be recompensed, so that you can at least find something similar. Another gold locket, for instance, that won't be identical to your original "find," but will also be a lovely antique.

How much is the premium? It will be based on value, and will vary according to the items listed and the town, city, or state in which you live. Insurance on sterling-silver flatware, for instance, generally costs about 50 cents per $100 value. Jewelry coverage in most parts of the country costs about $1 to $2 per $100 of value. In high-risk areas, however, this coverage might cost more. (And "high risk" might be a wealthy neighborhood where there are valuables that attract burglars.) In New York City the cost could be from $2.10 to $2.60 per $100; in Los Angeles the cost could be closer to $3 per $100. These figures are approximate or base prices; they may vary by the time you read this. Furthermore, some companies set their own premiums, which may be higher or

## Saving Money On Insurance

*You can save money on insurance by keeping your valuables in a safe-deposit box. If you are content just to know you have a collection, without being able to look at it whenever you feel like it, this is a possibility. You can go to the bank periodically and look at your goods in the area the bank provides for owners of safe-deposit boxes. Or you can leave your sterling flatware in the box and take it out only when your cousin the duchess is coming to dine—at which point you should also take out a short-term binder policy that will cover you until you put the silver back in the box.*

*But even in the safe-deposit box, you still need some insurance because many bank safe-deposit vaults either are not automatically insured against losses from burglary, fire, and floods, or have only minimal insurance. It's something you should check with your bank. So ultimately, whether in the bank or in your home, the protection you have is the policy that you buy.*

*Just to give my personal viewpoint, however, I believe that life is short and the things you own should be kept where they can be admired and even used—especially if they are adequately insured.*

lower than others, so it will pay you to shop around for the best coverage at the best price. Your own insurance broker or agent should be able to give you information about what's valuable at what price.

The personal articles floater does have some limitations. If it contains a "pair and set" clause (and most do), this clause limits the coverage on certain items to the *difference* between the cash value of the pair or set, and the cash value of what's left after the loss. Let's say, for instance, that you have a set of five sterling serving pieces, antiques and irreplaceable. Each of them is worth $500, but as matching pieces in a set they have a combined value, because they are a set, of $5000. If one is lost, the insurance company is liable afterwards for only $3000, the difference between $5000 when the set was intact and the value of the remaining pieces, four at $500 each or $2000. The same principle would apply to a pair of earrings. Admittedly, you can't wear a single earring, but you haven't lost the entire set if you've lost just one. (Someday I hope to start an exchange among people who have just one earring.)

Another fact you should know: Personal articles floaters automatically cover newly acquired items for only thirty days, may have dollar limits on them and may be restricted to covering only the type of property you already have covered, for instance, jewelry. After the thirty-day period the value of your new purchase has to be assessed or established, the item specifically listed, and the premiums adjusted. In other words, if you already have a personal articles floater and you acquire something new, you must, within thirty days, let your insurance agent know what you've bought and that you want it insured. Because you're listing something new, your premium will then be "adjusted" (the insurance industry's euphemism for *raised*).

One way to establish the value of your purchase, or purchases, is with your bill of sale, so you'll want to hold onto it and file it in a safe place. In some cases, you may need to have certain items appraised, especially if they were bargains, to be sure they are being insured for their current value. You may also want previous purchases appraised for the same reason. If you do get a rare find, in an antique necklace for example, and discover that it's worth much more than you paid for it at the auction, you'll need it insured at its true value.

All of this means you will probably want some kind of on-going inventory of your valuables. In addition to a written inventory, it's an excellent idea to have an inventory of color photographs. The photographs would also be useful should you ever decide to resell anything. In this way, you could prove that any repairs or damages on an item were there when you bought it, and not something

### The Question of Appraisals

*All appraisals must be* in writing *from a recognized source. You can't get an informal free appraisal from an auction house, write the figure down on a piece of paper, and use it for insurance purposes. Auction houses charge a fee for written appraisals, since you are drawing on their time and their expertise. Different houses use different standards for setting the fee, depending on the location, the number of items to be appraised, and the special expertise that might be needed. You will, of course, inquire about the fee before you make a commitment.*

*The American Society of Appraisers believes that an hourly or flat fee is more equitable than a fee that is a percentage of the value of the item. The Society sometimes considers the practice of charging a percentage fee unethical, and may use this practice as grounds for expelling a member. The reason is as follows: An appraiser may be tempted to put much too high a value on an object if he or she is going to get a percentage of the final total. It's tempting to do so, especially in the antique field where the value is difficult to set in absolute terms. How can someone state, unequivocally, that an antique is worth such and such when there is no exact duplicate to estimate it against or to set the price?*

that happened recently, which might spoil the value of the piece as an antique. You should have two sets of written inventory and photographs. Keep one either with your lawyer or in your safe-deposit box, the other with your insurance agent.

Once you've taken care of this inventory, the temptation will be to put it away and forget about it. There are lots of things to do that are more fun than continuously fussing with an inventory of your possessions. Sad to say, it's vitally important for you to keep it up to date. You should set up some kind of reminder so that at regular intervals you will recheck the inventory with your insurance agent to be sure you're keeping current on new values.

Floaters must be renewed every year and that's probably good, since renewing is an obvious reminder that you should check your coverage. At that time, you can change the amount of your coverage up or down, depending on what's happened to the market.

### The Really Bad News

Now let's get really gloomy, and talk about what happens if you do have a loss. Let's say that your home has been burglarized or that while you were traveling, your favorite antique bracelet or cuff links were stolen. At that particular moment, you are not necessarily your most calm and rational self, and you don't always do what you should do—which is to call the police.

You should call or go to the police even if you believe they haven't the slightest intention of coming around to investigate, and even if they are so accustomed to burglaries that it's hard for them to be more than minimally polite. It's important for you to call the police so that you can establish a loss for your income taxes. For the same reason, it's also important to call them if you notice, after some time has elapsed, that more items are missing than you first reported. If you don't call, Uncle Sam may say that you can't take a deduction for the loss because you didn't report it.

Since insurance terms vary because state laws vary, it's a good idea to discuss this whole question of theft with your insurance agent, perhaps even before you buy a policy. Then you can also learn what kind of coverage you have between the time you pick up the item that you buy at the auction and the time you get it back to your house, particularly good to know if you're buying at an out-of-town auction. Check on the kind of documentation you may need to prove your ownership at some future time. (You may also want these records to prove ownership for the items you're going to pass on to your heirs.)

Of course, you can't be insured against every unpleasant possibility, and you will ordinarily not have to face these questions. But for your own peace of mind you should check your insurance—and then not have to worry further.

# PART THREE

# THE SELLING SIDE
# OF THE GAME

# 12 SO YOU WANT TO SELL, NOT BUY

Now let's take a look at the other side of the auction scene. You don't want to buy at an auction—you want to sell through an auction house. What you want to sell could range from a single painting to some fine jewelry or antique furniture, to a portion of your household goods. You might even want to sell an entire estate, from the pots and pans in the kitchen to the house and grounds themselves.

Your reasons for selling would vary, of course, depending on what you want to sell. You might inherit something—jewelry, paintings, china, glassware—that has no sentimental value for you, but which you believe is valuable. You might decide (along with many other people these days) that in view of the rising crime rate, it's becoming too risky to hold onto such valuables as sterling silver and jewelry and that you should just cash them in, especially since the market for them has appreciated in recent years. You might decide it's time to upgrade your art collection (perhaps acquired at auctions) now that you are more knowledgeable, richer, or interested in realizing a profit on your earlier purchases. On a broader scale, there are sometimes major changes in our lives that almost require the decision to sell: death in the family, divorce, a move from one area of the country to another, or from a large house to a smaller home or apartment.

Whatever your reason for wanting to sell through an auction house, the better informed you are about the way such an operation works, the better your chances of getting a fair price for what you're selling.

### Checking Out the Market

In the two following chapters, we'll examine full-scale estate sales. Here we'll consider smaller, mostly single, items. How can you get an idea of the price they might bring in the current auction market? By doing some "comparison shopping," checking a variety of sources. Which sources you check will depend on what you're interested in selling. Here are some suggestions.

1. Go to retail stores and note the current prices for similar new items, such as fine furniture reproductions, or sterling tea and coffee sets, or jewelry.

2. Go to local antique dealers, who may be willing either to quote a price for buying the item outright, or to accept it on consignment, that is, to try to sell it for you within a given period of time, for an agreed-upon percentage of the selling price, or commission.

3. Send away for catalogs of future auctions that include items similar to those you are interested in selling, since, as you know, these catalogs often include presale estimates. Regard the price of the catalog—anywhere from $5 to $50 or more—as an investment. As I've noted,

*191*

many auction houses, if you ask, will also send to you, *after* an auction, the actual selling prices.

4. Go to the presale exhibitions of auctions of articles similar to the ones you want to sell. You can compare these items with your own and can ask the auction house aides what they estimate the pieces will go for.

5. Go to the actual auctions that are selling similar items. Again, you can compare the condition of these items with yours and you can see the prices they get.

6. Go to the free appraisal days offered by many auction houses, and get estimates on your items from their experts.

7. Call and arrange for an appraisal from a local auction house. Many people believe that you can get such appraisals only during certain designated, publicized days, but this isn't so. If you have something that you

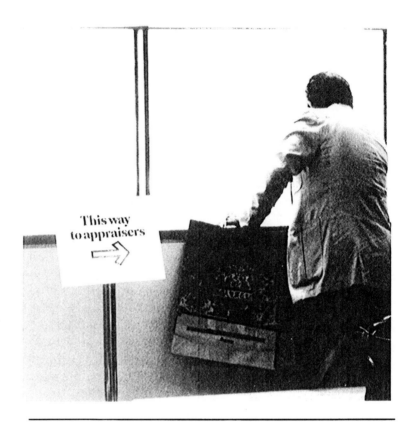

think is valuable, you can call an auction house, discuss the item on the phone with the resident expert, and if the person believes it is valuable, he or she will often arrange an individual appointment at a mutually convenient time. An initial call is always a good idea, since telephone description sometimes is enough for you to learn that a particular item has little resale value, saving both you and the auction house time and trouble.

For instance, I got very excited when I saw a hammered sterling-silver cream and sugar set in an auction house display case, because the hammered pattern was similar to the pattern on two small silver baskets we had found in my mother-in-law's house. When I called Plaza

193

Galleries in New York City and spoke to Douglas Reymer, an expert there who had appraised some jewelry for me, and told him about the mark on the baskets, *Made in U.S.A.,1* and the glimpses of copper through the silver, he told me with some regret that they were not sterling, and not very valuable. (Another dream of new-found riches gone in a pouff!)

8. If you can't get to the auction house because you're too busy, it's too far, or the item you want to sell is too big or too heavy to be easily transported—a large piece of furniture, for instance—mail a photograph to the auction house with an explanatory letter telling as much as you know that's pertinent about the history of the piece (that your grandmother brought it with her from Europe, your uncle bought it when he was stationed in India in World War II). The auction house will write and give you an estimate of whether or not the item might be salable at auction. (Such estimates are not formal enough to be used for insurance purposes.)

In checking these auction sources, you are getting not only some idea about the value of your item, but also some idea about how well the auction house is run. This second level of information can be important in helping you choose which auction house to do business with, either for the single item you are now considering or perhaps, at some other time, for handling a major sale. (Of course, you're also learning values when you're on the other side of the auction transaction, buying.)

*Finding the Right Auction House*

Now for a look at the inevitable psychological over-tones, so often lurking in the background when we talk about our possessions. First, the bad news. You are likely to experience a certain amount of disillusionment when you take in some family heirloom to be appraised. The stories of their ostensible value are often passed down

along with the possessions, and could easily be exaggerated (from sentiment or lack of knowledge rather than by design). Your mother remembers that that coffee pot was given to her by an aunt who bought only the best of everything, so it *must* be sterling. Those candlesticks or that kettle has been in the family for years; everyone knows how valuable antiques are, so they must be worth a lot of money.

Brace yourself. The sterling pot may be silver plate; the candlesticks and kettle are attractive, but there are a lot of them on the market and they really are not worth very much. You may actually be quite shaken up when you learn the true value of the items you want to sell. You won't *want* to believe what you hear, because it will undo some treasured family myths. In such cases, re-

*195*

member that although there is no dollar price on sentiment, these things still have a value to you as part of your
family's heritage.

Now for the good news. Some of the items that are
lying around in desk drawers or hidden in closets may be
worth a good deal more than you thought. And even if
you don't receive thousands of dollars, should you decide
to put the items up for auction, you will still get money
that you would not have had otherwise. Consider the
case of a gold watch that belonged to my husband's father as a fairly typical example of what can happen.

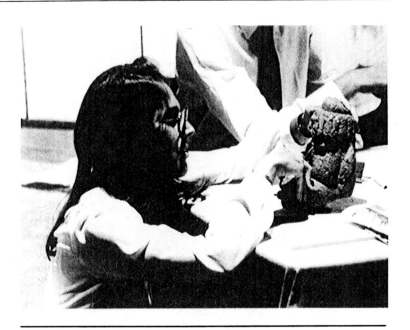

When I became interested in auctions, my husband and I began to look around, speculatively, at some of the antiques we had. He remembered a gold pocket watch that had belonged to his father, which had been sitting in his desk drawer for about thirty years. The watch had no meaning to our children, since they had never known their grandfather. We decided to sell it, and I took it first to a neighborhood antique dealer who has a well-deserved reputation for astuteness and honesty. He offered us $225 if he bought it outright, but said he thought he could sell it, although he couldn't promise when, for about $325, from which he would take a ten percent commission. Other dealers I checked with estimated a somewhat higher price but asked for commissions that varied from twenty to fifty percent. (Dealers' commissions vary considerably, so these figures are not necessarily what a dealer in your area would charge.)

My next stop was one of New York's most prestigious auction houses. (Nothing is too good for the working class!) One of their jewelry experts put the watch down on a glass case absolutely glittering with that week's exhibition—the diamond, emerald, ruby, sapphire, gold and platinum jewelry of various movie stars, Countess this, and Mrs. Tycoon that. My poor little watch almost shriveled up inside its case with all those gorgeous things nearby.

Mr. F. picked up the watch gingerly, somewhat in the manner of a housewife picking up a dead mouse by its tail, examined it, and then looked at me hesitantly. I said, "Don't worry, I won't be offended by what you say." I thought I meant it when I said it, but I was kidding myself. My feelings really *were* hurt when he said, very summarily, "I think it might fetch about $400, but we really wouldn't even deal with such things here. You'll have to take it to our other gallery"—the one, in other words, that handles things of lesser quality.

So I took the watch there, somewhat warily. They, too, said it would fetch about $400. But still feeling put down, I decided to move on.

The next auction house said they thought the watch would fetch about $350, but they weren't sure. They were quite polite and didn't pick up the watch *quite* so gingerly—more as if they were accustomed to (but not too happy about) handling turquoise and pearls as well as emeralds and diamonds. Still, I thought I'd get one more opinion.

I noticed that a smaller house had many jewelry auctions. (I later found out they auctioned off more jewelry than any other house in the world.) I called and described the watch on the phone: fourteen-carat gold, engraved, running and in excellent condition. Their young jewelry expert, Mr. R., said, "It sounds like a very nice watch. Bring it over right away." As you can see, though I tried to deny it, and though my husband and I had decided together that we had many other family mementos more precious to us than a watch that hadn't even been looked at in many years, there still were feelings and emotions and, yes, status, at work. I wanted a little appreciation for the quality of something that *belonged* to us. Making the final decision to sell was not easy. However, the young man turned out to be charming and gracious, said the watch was beautiful, and that he thought he could say, conservatively, that it would probably fetch about $250 to $300, and perhaps more. I decided on the spot to put it up for auction with his house.

Incidentally, I had a nice surprise when he came out of the examining room. The watch had not been looked at for years, and when Mr. R. opened it with a jeweler's tool, he found a photograph of my husband's mother and father. I took the photograph home and left the watch, after signing a contract (more about this below) and buying insurance for $5. I said I would, of course, come to the auction taking place about nine weeks from the present date, which was August 7th.

Notice that time lapse, from August 7th to October 8th. Why October 8th? That was the date for auctioning other jewelry and watches, and therefore the date when the best audience of dealers and private buyers and collectors would be on hand to bid. And so it was the date when I was most likely to get the best price. (The watch actually sold to a private collector for $525. After deducting $5 for insurance and $52.50 for the ten-percent commission, we received a check for $467.50 a little more than a month after the date of the sale.)

## Signing the Contract

I've already mentioned that I signed a contract with the auction house. That is the last step in assigning some of your goods for sale. Since the contract sets out the responsibilities of both you and the auction house, you need to examine it carefully so you're sure you understand the terms. Here are some of the points you should check on, hidden as they may be among all the "aforementioneds" and "whereases" and "heretofores" that

are dear to the hearts of lawyers who write such contracts.

1. What commission must you pay? It may be a ten-percent "seller's fee" common at New York City auctions where a ten-percent *buyer's* fee is also the rule. Or it may range from twenty to thirty percent where there are no buyer's fees. The rate also varies considerably depending on what's being auctioned, how much and what kind of work is involved, the area of the country, and the individual auctioneer. Obviously, there is much more work involved in running an auction sale of the contents of a large home than in auctioning several pieces of furniture that the owner himself delivers to an auction house, and the commission might vary accordingly.

Now, auctioneers say publicly that their rate is not negotiable and, when talking privately, urge each other never to cut rates. But the fact is that rates *are* negotiable. People with very valuable collections or large estates—especially if they are well known, so their names would lend prestige to the auction house—are in a particularly good position to negotiate commissions. Lesser mortals can at least attempt it; it's always possible to pay more, if the auction house says no.

Caution: A low commission rate should not be the only basis for choosing an auctioneer. There are many criteria, as you will see.

2. What kind of insurance will cover your property? For what period of time? What will the cost be?

3. Will your consigned piece be featured in the auctioneer's catalog? If so, who pays? For many auction houses, only the more important sales are promoted through these lovely glossy catalogs with color photographs. It surprised me to learn that for some houses, the *seller* may have to pay for having an item pictured in the catalog. There are exceptions. If you happen to own a diamond tiara that once held a princess's hair in place and you've decided to part with it (they're not wearing them this year), you won't have to pay to have it featured.

4. Will you have to pay for packing and shipping or trucking the items to the auction house, if you can't deliver them personally? If so, how much?

5. Should your contract set a reserve on the article or articles? If so, how high? A reserve, you'll remember, is the confidential minimum price agreed upon between the seller and the auction house. Different auction houses give different advice or have different standards for what the reserve should be. Generally, it is fixed at or about the low estimate for the piece, but the reserve may be about forty percent of the estimate if the estimate is $500 or lower, or about sixty-six percent of the estimate if it's above $500.

Some auction houses also charge a fee for allowing a

## An Emotion–Filled Business

*The business of being in the auction sale catalog can be very touchy. One of my favorite auctioneers, president of his prestigious company and a lovely gentleman, told me about a widow who took it for granted that her husband's desk would be in the catalog. She was so hurt when it was not that she asked to have the desk returned after it had been sold! The auctioneer, going beyond the call of business or duty found out who had bought the desk, got in touch with the buyer, and explained the situation. The buyer was sympathetic, and the auctioneer, at his own expense, had the desk returned to the widow. Auctioneering can be a very personal, emotion-filled business.*

seller to place a reserve, since the house may have to protect the reserve by having someone on their staff take part in the bidding. If the bidding doesn't reach the estimate, the house will have to recall the article, doing what is popularly known as "buying back" or "buying in." If the house does have to buy in or buy back, you will still have to pay a commission, but it will be less than if the article had been sold; five percent is fairly typical. (Incidentally, these charges are usually not paid out in advance but are deducted from the final price before you as the seller are paid.)

Auctioneers understandably prefer to have unreserved auctions. It's an enormous amount of work to put an auction together, so they like to sell every item when it is offered and go on to the next one. In fact, some auctioneers don't accept reserves. (Auctioneers will confess privately that they love estate sales for a deceased owner, especially if ordered by a bank or trust company, since there are no reserves and no withholding of property.) The auction-goer also is probably better off at an unreserved auction, since there is always the opportunity to get a real bargain, without that prearranged minimum.

But as a seller, you may have a different viewpoint:

You don't want your property to be sold for too low a price. On the other hand, you may share the auctioneer's feeling that since you've decided to sell, you'd like to see the item go. There are no hard and fast rules as to which is better. It's an individual decision that you have to make, depending on the article, the circumstances, and your own feelings.

A final point: There is, of course, always the possibility of having someone go to the auction and bid on your behalf, in order to keep the bidding going and to help you get a good price. Auctioneers consider this unethical, on the grounds that this means the auction is not "open" to everyone on the same basis. However, it is a way of giving your property some protection, though you run the risk of ending up buying back your own property, and even having to pay the buyer's premium. And it certainly happens at some auctions.

So far, we've been talking mostly about auctioning off one or a few items. Having an *estate* auction—disposing of either your own or someone else's household goods—presents a different range of questions and problems, and that's what we'll look at next.

# 13 WHAT YOU SHOULD KNOW ABOUT ESTATE SALES

What's almost as inevitable as death and taxes? A time when you are faced with the problem of disposing of all or a major portion of your own or someone else's possessions or "estate."

I put that word "estate" in quotes because it brings to mind (at least to my mind) the picture of a huge stone house, imperiously set on perfect, deep-green lawns (no dandelion dares raise a yellow head!) surrounded by 300-year-old trees, every leaf in place. It ain't necessarily so. An estate is everything someone owns: all real property, minus debts and obligations.

These days, with the breakup of families through divorce and the moves from one part of the country to another, or from large homes to smaller ones, many of us face the problem of disposing of our personal property.

And for most of us, there also comes a time when we have to dispose of the estate of a parent or relative. In either instance, we are faced with the problem of how to dispose of our own or someone else's worldly goods— from the smaller possessions of everyday life to the house and grounds, even if they're not huge mansions in story-book settings.

In general, you have several options: a tag sale, a sale to a dealer, or a professional auction, run either on the auctioneer's premises or at your home or even apartment. Two major factors will influence your choice: time, including how much of your own time would be involved, because your time is worth money; and the net amount of money you'd get after expenses were paid.

### Tag Sales, Dealers, Auctions: Pros and Cons

Let's look briefly at the advantages and disadvantages of the tag sale and the sale to a dealer, then move on to consider auction sales in more detail.

If you choose a tag sale, which is a sale at your home with all the items *tagged* with their price, you can either hire a professional tag-sale company or individual to determine the prices and administer the whole operation, or you can do it yourself. If you choose to do it yourself, you'll need to know the value or market for each item, which requires an expertise that few of us have. If you hire a professional, you must pay a commission, usually between twenty-five and thirty percent. The pros and cons of a tag sale are clear: You have the *possibility* of doing well, but you have no guarantees since a tag sale can be affected by factors over which you have no control: weather, news of the economy around the time of your sale, competing events, rival sales. On the other hand, the money is yours, quickly, once the sale is held.

Now let's consider the pluses and minuses of selling to a dealer. The pluses first: less of your time involved, a fixed price, fast removal, and quick payment. As with the

tag sale, this quick payment can be used immediately to pay bills or to earn interest in a bank account or dividends from some form of investment. The drawback? The main disadvantage is that you must accept the dealer's valuations and *his* price. The dealer, for his part, must make a profit large enough to cover expenses, from his own salary to the money tied up holding onto your things until they are sold. If he can increase that profit by buying your things very cheaply, he will. He is in no way obliged to tell you the market value of what you own—and he won't. He's not in business for fun or recreation, but for the money.

So much for tag sales and dealers—each, in certain circumstances, a perfectly reasonable way of selling estates. What about our third choice, consigning the estate to an auction house?

Like everything else, an auction house has its advantages and disadvantages. First the solid good news. The auction house, customarily at no charge, will send someone to your home to *estimate* what your property will

206

bring at auction, so you have some idea of its value. The estimate will be done by specialists, and will be based not only on their knowledge of the various items involved (paintings, furniture, silverware), but also on what similar pieces have brought at auction fairly recently—in other words, the current market. The auction house will then handle the sale for you, either removing your property to its gallery where it will be auctioned, or operating a sale directly on the premises. Furthermore, the house may separate your property into various categories—furniture, paintings, rugs, books—and offer each type of goods at specialized auction sales that attract collectors and dealers, likely to be the customers who are most interested and will offer the best prices.

If the auction people handle a house sale for you, they will organize it from start to finish (with the proper contract), relieving you of much responsibility. (More on the contract shortly.) And you can put a reserve on most items—the minimum price that you must get, under which you will refuse to sell.

What about the drawbacks? The primary drawback is, from another angle, the major reason you just might *want* to go the auction route. This is the fact that no one, of course, can guarantee the total amount of money you will realize at an auction. As with tag sales, there is that element of chance, and any number of factors, ranging from the weather to the fickleness of people's tastes, to their feelings about the stability of the world on the day (or days) you ask them to open their pocketbooks or wallets, to the ability of the auctioneer, can lower the final amount. But conversely, there is always the possibility of doing surprisingly well. And this is the hope that makes auctions so tempting.

Reputable auctioneers will tell you they really don't know what may happen to prices at an auction, though they usually have a reasonably sound expectation based on their knowledge of the market. But the unexpected can always happen. When Christie's auctioned the contents of Dunford, the Long Island home of Mrs. Mary Sanford, widow of millionaire Stephen Sanford (Sanford carpets and the Sanforized process), back in September 1980, the big surprise was the price for ten only slightly erotic canvases of female nudes, which had a presale estimate of $200 to $300. In an otherwise slightly somnolent auction, to an audience that included many dressed in tennis outfits, or Calvin Klein jeans and Gucci shoes, the appearance of these drawings brought forth a sudden outburst of "woo-woos!" and very spirited bidding. Mike Capo, a twenty-seven-year-old Manhattan dealer, bid loud and clear (nothing subtle about his bidding style) against a dealer who stayed unidentified. Mike told me later that he had wanted five of the nudes to hang in his bathroom and five to give to a friend. But he dropped out when the bidding reached $1700. In another minute, the paintings went to the anonymous dealer for $1800.

Who knows? Someone might come along and fall in love with that clock you've kept on the mantle all these years, even though you hated it, because it was a wedding present from your only rich relative. Even better, maybe *two* people will fall in love with it and bid fiercely against each other. Sad to say, however, some of the things that you love so much will get no more than a yawn or a "what-did-they-ever-see-in-that" look. Taking the auction option is also taking a chance emotionally.

A few additional considerations. Needless to say, the auction house will invest much time and effort in handling your sale; they expect to be paid for this investment of time and money through a commission. The commission will vary, depending on the individual auctioneer and the going rate in the part of the country where you live. It can range from a ten-percent seller's fee in the areas where the buyer also pays a ten-percent buyer's fee, to twenty to thirty percent if no buyer's fee is charged. (Beyond the commission, an auction house will also bill you for some services, such as transportation, insurance, and advertising.)

Finally, you have to allow for a time lapse from the date you sign your contract with the auctioneer to the date you get your share of the proceeds. There are various reasons for this. Your auction has to be fitted into the auctioneer's schedule. Some of your possessions may belong in a specialized auction of pottery and porcelain, for instance, or rugs, and the auction house will (with your permission) hold these things until that auction, which might not be for several months. And different houses have different systems for paying, from one week to thirty-five days or more after the auction date.

### Where to Hold the Auction

You've decided to take the auction route. Now you've got one more decision: Should the sale be handled at the auction house or at your own home? There are (as usual) pluses and minuses to each possibility. On the plus side of the sale at the auction house: its status or prestige, which may attract a more well-to-do audience willing to pay higher prices; its location, which may attract more buyers, particularly those people who are regular followers of that auction house (the "drop-in" audience); its ability to place special items in specialized auctions which, as mentioned before, are most likely to attract the highly interested dealers and collectors.

On the minus side: the time involved while your things are picked up, properly tagged for identification, scheduled, entered into a catalog. There's the possibility of damage in transit or at the auction house, and mixups with other consignments. And needless to say, every lag in selling the goods means a corresponding lag in getting paid.

What about the pluses and minuses of house sales? According to auctioneers, on the plus side is the "sentiment factor." Neighbors will come and will often pay more than a stranger would, because they want a remembrance from the house. Next, there is in some cases the status factor: people in the area (not neighbors in the sense of friends) will buy something because they want to own an item that once belonged to someone who lived nearby and was very rich or chic or famous for a variety of reasons. (Buyers came from the neighborhood and from far away to bid on the contents of a brothel, Pam's Purple Door, South Dakota. See next page.) A festive air can surround a house auction, especially if the weather is fine, an atmosphere that provides the perfect breeding ground for an especially virulent auction-fever bug. At such a sale, the occasional auction-goer with little appreciation of value, caught up in the action, may bid up the prices, to the despair of dealers and the delight of the consignor. (Something to remember when you're buying, not selling!)

One auctioneer who specializes in house sales told me that the estate auction of someone well liked who has died will always bring out a contingent of neighbors and handkerchiefs. The neighbors will shake their heads as the coffee set and fine china from which they often drank and ate goes on the block; they will sigh as the couches and chairs they sat upon come up; they'll reach for their handkerchiefs as they see the antique clock whose chimes reminded them it was time to go home. "They weep," he says, "but they go right on bidding."

On the minus side of the house sale is the somewhat limited audience—many dealers and collectors won't come unless there are some really rare and special items on sale; and the possibility of bad weather—a hot spell or rain—which can severely hurt a house auction. A more complex problem is the mix of valuable and not-so-valuable goods, which can affect the sale sometimes unpredictably. The mix of worthwhile and inconsequential may raise the overall price level, or it may lower the level. If people perceive that some of the items being offered are not of high quality, they may underbid on those things that are actually very fine. (Again, something to remember when you're buying.) Finally, if there is an

## Fun And Feathers at A Most Unlikely Auction

*Lead, South Dakota—population 1,794—was the scene of a local-industry auction that's not likely to be repeated anywhere else in the United States. On July 17, 1980, more than one thousand men and women from the surrounding area and more distant parts of the country, as well as the media (CBS and NBC were there, as was* Time *magazine, and reporters from the local papers) came to Lead to ogle, and to bid on the contents of Pam's Purple Door. It was one of several bordellos that had been operating for about a century despite the state's antiprostitution laws; state authorities had finally closed all of them.*

*Local residents who opposed shutting down what* Time *magazine called "some of the best little whorehouses in the West" held protest parades; the men in fancy buckskin on foot and horseback, the women in décolleté dresses that would have pleased Pam's former customers. But to no avail, and Pam Holliday, proprietess of Pam's Purple Door, said she had to auction off her property to help pay her lawyer's fees. (Owners and employees of the houses had been taken into custody as material witnesses in a federal grand jury probe.)*

*In promoting the auction, held at the local armory, the handbills noted, "This large auction could very well be the final curtain on an era of Historic Deadwood and Black Hills history that has lasted over 100 years. Because of the circumstances involved, every item is a collectible."*

*The auctioneers wore purple feathers in their straw cowboy hats and of course amused the crowd by asking bidders, "How do you know so much about that?" Some 517 individuals registered to bid (a record for local auctions), saying they were buying either "a piece of history," souvenirs, or items that would someday be valuable. Those who weren't bidding could still spend money on T-shirts sold by the local chamber of commerce, imprinted "I Was There: Pam's Purple Door Auc-* 🖝

*tion." About 500 were sold during the day, for $7.50 each, and another 144 had been sold before the auction even started. People could also take time off from bidding to get Pam to autograph auction handbills, at $2 per autograph.*

*When the auction began, about 4:30 in the afternoon, the bleachers and the floor were nearly full and the bidding was lively. One man paid $17.50 for a metal wall plaque similar to those sold in local tourist souvenir shops for $1.50. Ordinary ten-cent-store figurines brought from $15 to $25. Some of the most sought-after items were oven timers, an electric vibrator pillow, and a crushed-velvet tiger-striped bedspread with matching curtains. A wooden plaque reading, "Save energy, sleep with a friend," brought $25; a collection of motel, car, and other keys, $25; Pam's teapot, $50; a small lamp on a hula-girl stand with a fancy red shade, $160; a wicker headboard, $150; and a set of purple sheets, $22. But by the time cocktail and dinner time rolled around, the crowd had diminished. Ashtrays that had sold earlier for $20 to $50 went for $5, and a twin bed with double mattress, in good condition, sold for $15.*

*When it was all over, about 1:00 a.m., the sale had netted Pam Holliday only several thousand dollars. But as Mary Lochridge, managing editor of the* Lead Daily Call, *commented in one of several lively stories about the auction, complete with pictures of Miss Holliday autographing purchases, "lots of diamonds on her fingers reveal that she has a long way to go before she's in the poorhouse."*

enormous amount of items to be sold, both large and small, and only one day to sell them, the auctioneer must maintain a rapid pace that sometimes doesn't allow time for the kind of competitive bidding that sends prices way up.

The long and the short of it, as you've gathered by

now, is that there is no way of setting firm rules on the best way to dispose of an estate. It depends on what you have to sell, where you live, the season of the year, the pressure from trust lawyers to settle, and so on. Situations differ, so choices differ, too. Your best bet is to review your situation and your objectives and then choose.

Once you've decided to go the auction route, however, you should know something about the components of a successful estate auction, so that you can choose a good auction house and help ensure that your property fetches the best prices. This is the topic we'll discuss next.

# 14

# HOW TO SELL AN ESTATE THROUGH AN AUCTION HOUSE

You've decided to sell an estate (yours or one that you're responsible for) by means of an auction, either on the premises or at an auction house. Now, how can you best protect your interests and help make the auction successful? As you'll see, you can be a very active participant in the proceedings.

*Choosing the Auction House*

It's important to hire an auctioneer who has a reputation for running an open and fair auction. Before you decide, you should, if you can, observe him or her in action—especially if you are planning an on-site sale. Local people need to know they will be recognized and treated fairly or else they are likely to tell their friends that such and such an auctioneer plays favorites, so don't bother to go to any auction he runs. Here is good advice on choosing an auctioneer from *The Auction Encyclopedia,* a book addressed to the profession: "The auctioneer's attitude toward people is very important. Watch how he and his associates handle themselves. . . . He should always be in control, yet have a good rapport with the crowd. . . . Watch how he starts the auction to see if he really takes charge and works the people well. . . . Keep in mind that what you are interested in is *the bottom line,* how much money the sale will produce. The auctioneer with the most professional voice may not be the auctioneer who gets the highest prices. The actual auctioneer's chant is not nearly as important as the auctioneer's ability to get *top dollar for property* [my italics] . . . ."

To which I add, go, listen, and observe the men and women who will be doing the auctioneering. Most importantly, whether they use the chanting style popular outside the major urban areas or the more "English" style of announcing the bids, can they be understood? Nothing turns an audience off faster, especially people who are not seasoned auction-goers, than an auctioneer who is hard to follow. It makes people worry that they don't know what's going on, and then, rather than take a chance on bidding for something they don't want or don't know the ongoing bids for, they sit on their hands or just leave.

Let me also add a personal bias. Auctioneers are encouraged to tell jokes, to keep the audience in a good humor. But there are jokes—and jokes. And there are still auctioneers in some parts of the country who are telling jokes that poke fun at women. These macho jokes turn me off, not only because I object as a woman but also because I think they're bad for business. Frequently the jokes portray women as "dumb broads" who are cute but don't understand a thing about money. Oddly enough, these jokes are often told by male auctioneers whose wives are their partners in the business, usually handling the company's finances!

Next you'll want to check on the auctioneer's status. If a license is required in your state, does he have one? You can find out if it's required by checking with your state, city, or county licensing bureau. Some states do not require an auctioneer's license, but in these cases, auctioneers must get permits from local towns, cities, or counties. You'll also want to know if he is bonded, since his employees will be handling your possessions and money, and if he has liability insurance, to protect against mishaps and accidents.

The people helping the auctioneer, sometimes known as "ring" men, should be experienced. As you know, they help the auctioneer spot potential bidders. And, of course, all the other people—clerks, moving men, cashiers—are important because they keep the auction going smoothly and maintain the records.

Incidentally, many auction houses are family affairs, with each member contributing some expertise from being specialists in fine arts to acting as cashiers. Such family enterprises, when well run, have a terrific operation.

### Checking Out the Contract

You will, of course, want a contract—and a contract that is specific. It should be written in understandable English, not legalese. There are two most welcome trends these days: contracts that are simplified so that ordinary intelligent people can read and understand them; and consumers who are not afraid to say, "I don't understand that. What does it mean?" Don't be embarrassed or shy about asking questions. Remember, it's your money and your time at stake. (If you have doubts, you might want to have an attorney look over the contract to be sure that your interests are being protected.)

A typical contract will contain the following points and information, listed here in abbreviated form:

1. A guarantee by the auctioneer to use his best skill in

preparing and conducting a sale. (Note that *preparing*—a very important part of a successful auction.)

2. A list of the property you are going to sell at auction.

3. A clause that says you will not withdraw or sell any items on this list before the auction, except by mutual consent between you and the auctioneer.

(Here's the reason for this clause. Prior to the auction, friends, relatives, and even dealers sometimes attempt to buy individual pieces, very often the best ones. Or you may decide to give away certain items of sentimental value to friends, relatives, and children. In both instances, the auctioneer would be left with the job of trying to make money for himself and for you from the less valuable goods. Understandably, he tries to protect himself against this contingency with the "nonwithdrawal" clause, and another related clause. If you withdraw or sell an item before the auction without notifying him, the contract specifies that you must pay the full commission to him for those pieces anyway.)

4. An agreement to postpone the auction, in case of bad weather, to a mutually agreeable date.

5. An agreement on whether or not various items will have a reserve; "will be protected" is a phrase also used. (If the decision on the reserve is not specified in the contract, you may want a separate written agreement so you both know what you've agreed on. Very often an auction house will not accept a reserve on items that it estimates will go for less than $500.)

6. A statement that the auctioneer can deduct his fee from the *gross* amount of the sale.

7. A statement that the auctioneer will give you the net proceeds from the auction, along with the sale records and the receipts. (These records and receipts are important, so that you can verify the auctioneer's claims as to what was sold, at what price, and even to whom, if you're curious about that.)

8. A statement that you really own what you say you own, and/or you have the right to sell it. (In legalese,

you state that you have "good title" and "the goods are free of encumbrances," such as some remaining installment payments on a TV set, for instance.)

9. A list of the services and costs that you agree to pay for, which might include, in addition to the auctioneer's fee, charges for clerks, cashiers, other personnel (moving men, for example), advertising, and, perhaps, "miscellaneous" or "other." (Several things to watch for here: You may want to put a dollar limit on the amount of money the auctioneer can spend for advertising. You will certainly want to check on how many additional people he thinks he needs and what they will cost. And you want specifics on that "miscellaneous" or "other.")

*Appraising Your Estate*

An appraiser from the auction house will come and give you some idea of the value of your goods. If you happen to have any antiques and can establish their authenticity by means of family records, old bills, statements of previous owners, and so on, by all means do so. It will benefit you and the auctioneer. If you don't have such proof, you will want to know how much background and expertise the auctioneer or his appraiser has for judging values. If there are no specialists on the staff, and you believe you have valuable antiques, works of art, jewelry, or whatever, ask the auctioneer to call experts (other auctioneers or collectors) who can give an accurate appraisal. Without accurate appraisals of antiques or collector's items, you risk losing hundreds or even thousands of dollars.

*Planning a House Auction*

Now let's discuss the details of an auction held at a home (on-site, as the auctioneers say). Auctioneers who handle house sales usually commit themselves to dispose of everything, but that doesn't mean that everything is

## The Different Types of Appraisals And Their Purposes

*An appraisal by an auction house differs distinctly from two other common types of appraisals—for insurance purposes and tax purposes. In the case of an appraisal for insurance purposes, the appraiser has to give a figure that represents the* replacement *value of the item, since the purpose of the insurance appraisal is to establish a dollar figure in case of loss. For taxes, the appraiser sets a figure that the Internal Revenue Service can use to determine the value of an estate and, therefore, the amount of estate taxes that are due. For a fee, auction houses will provide such an appraisal, in writing and duly notarized. (The fee is sometimes refunded if, within a given period of time, the goods are consigned to the auction house to be auctioned.)*

*The type of auction-house appraisal we're concerned with here is an* oral estimate, *given by a specialist from the auction house—but a specialist on* auction prices. *Such an estimate* cannot *be used for insurance or tax purposes, since the appraiser is stating, based on his knowledge of the market, what he believes the estate would bring if sold at auction. Generally, this estimate is free, since the auctioneer hopes that you will consign the estate to him, especially if it's valuable.*

*As you might expect, there is a conflict of viewpoints between the wish of an estate executor to keep values low, in order to keep estate taxes low, and the wish of heirs auctioning off estates to get as much as possible, to have immediate cash. It is an issue you might want to discuss with an accountant or tax lawyer.*

*salable.* So you may have to face a fact of life that, auctioneers tell me, is sometimes difficult for clients to accept. (And, from what I've heard from a number of families, is sometimes more easily accepted by some family members than others.) The appraisal may not be what you expect, and you have to be realistic, maybe even persuade others to be realistic, about values.

As the auctioneer looks over the property, he may even suggest that some items have so little sale value that they would only cheapen the auction. He may recommend (and he may very well be right) that you simply take what is not salable, give it to charity, and get a receipt for the value so you can claim it as a deduction on your income tax.

Of course, the reverse can happen, too. The appraiser may look at your property and discover that something is far more valuable than you had thought. Russell E. Burke III, of Sloan's in Washington, went to examine a Boston estate and to pick up a painting by John Singer Sargent. Mr. Burke is an authority on paintings, and while he was looking around, he noticed another canvas that seemed valuable. The family told him an appraiser had put a value of $1,500 on it. But when Mr. Burke examined it carefully, he noted that it was signed and dated—the work of the Dutch artist Salomon van Ruisdael. The painting fetched $185,000 at Sloan's on September 23, 1979.

But remember: An estimate or appraisal, as all reputable auctioneers will tell you, is only an *estimate,* although very often it is close to the mark. No one can give you an absolute firm price. You know the final price only when an object is "knocked down" on the auction block; until that moment, everything is estimate or "guesstimate."

### Promoting a House Auction

Experienced auctioneers know that one key to a successful house auction is the display of the items to be auctioned—so, of course, you'll want to discuss that with the auctioneer. If feasible, items should be grouped so that they suggest to buyers how they might be used. A dining table, for instance, might have a tablecloth on it and be set with dishes, glasses, vases, silver. Chairs, lamps, and end tables might be grouped together in a setting for conversation, suggesting that buyers take the

## Good Times And Great Prices: A Splendiferous "House" Sale

*One of the most elegant and profitable estate auctions of recent days was held in May 1980 at a splendid summer home in Cambridge, on Maryland's eastern shore. The country estate being auctioned had belonged to Colonel and Mrs. Edgar William Garbisch.*

*Mrs. Garbisch had been Bernice Chrysler, second daughter of Walter Chrysler, the automotive magnate, when she married Colonel Garbisch, a former all-American football player from La Porte, Indiana. The Garbisches spent almost fifty years together, enjoying their passion for collecting American furniture, American folk art, Chinese export porcelain, eighteenth-century French furniture, French Impressionist and modern paintings, and European ceramics. Some of their ceramics, French furniture, and paintings decorated their small but elegant apartment in the posh Carlyle Hotel on New York's Madison Avenue. They spent the summers at their country estate, Pokety Farms, on Maryland's eastern shore, and it was here that they kept their magnificent collection of American furniture, folk art, and Chinese porcelain.*

*Much of the collection was bequeathed to their two children and to museums, but enough remained to allow for a grand auction. The main auctioneer, as befitted such a distinguished and gala affair—to say nothing of the quality of the goods on the block—was Sotheby's president, John Marion, who with no difficulty managed to run up a $4 million total by the time he'd brought down his gavel for the last bid.*

*Had you been invited to bid on the possessions of the Colonel and his wife, you probably would have sailed up to Pokety Farms in your sailboat, and after docking it, proceeded directly to the main tent. You would have mingled under the great tent with many private collectors and with some of the outstanding dealers of the country, many of whom had originally sold some of the items to the Garbisches. If you were planning to do a lot of entertaining, you might have bid for a set of* ☛

*Chinese porcelain, but since you hadn't decided to go as high as $45,000, you would have lost out to a private Connecticut collector who bid by phone and won.*

*In fact, many of the winning bids at the auction came via telephone from private collectors, who thereby missed all the fun. Then again, this arrangement might have been better for their figures, since Sotheby's offered fabulous buffet lunches during the several days when ten thousand or more people came to look, to bid, to enjoy the view of Chesapeake Bay, and in general to share in the good times.*

*The highest price paid at this sale, which set a new record for American furniture, was $250,000 for the "extremely rare and important Chippendale block and shell carved Cuban mahogany kneehole desk, possibly by Edmond Townsend, Newport, Rhode Island, 1760 to 1780." The desk was sold to a private American collector, who also bid by telephone. Bernard Levy, a well-known New York City antique dealer, had sold the desk in 1959 for $18,500 and then again in 1962 for $45,000. The Garbisches, who had been unwilling to buy it at the first price of $18,500, did buy it when it came on the block at an estate sale, for $125,000. Mr. Levy bid $240,000 on it, but lost it to the private collector.*

*John Walton, another dealer, was acting as agent at the sale for a client who had turned down a rare Queen Anne walnut-backed stool from Rhode Island when Mr. Walton had it in his shop at $1,700. It was bought at that time by the Garbisches. Mr. Walton bid $19,000 and won it for the client who had regretted losing the chair so many years earlier.*

*If you didn't want to spend so much, there were items you could buy for under $5,000: a wafering iron (used to seal letters and such) with a rare eagle design, $1,000; a small early American rug, $3,600; a quilt used in the guest bedroom, $3,500. Admittedly, there weren't many of these bargains around.*

*At the conclusion of the sale, Sotheby's also got the*

*assignment to sell the estate itself. So, if you weren't interested in furnishings and you had $3 million to spare, you could come back and at least bid on Pokety, with its three and a half miles of shoreline, coves, marshes, and a mile-long walled lagoon for winter waterfowl. Plus stables, a pasture, a sixty-foot swimming pool, an indoor bowling alley, a greenhouse, kennels, and a two-slip pier for boats.*

*In all, the affair was a huge success in terms of money and very favorable press.*

whole group. Fine crystal and cut glass should be put where the sun will shine on it, or displayed where it can be lighted, so it will sparkle. The smart auctioneer understands very well the importance of showmanship in having a good sale.

You should find out how much and what kind of advance advertising the auctioneer plans, first because you may be billed for it, and second because you may want to check the copy to be sure it's accurate. I have been very annoyed by auction ads that promise more than they deliver. They have made me hesitate before going again to auctions run by these auctioneers. So if you have the time, look at the advertising, whether it's a flyer, an ad in a local paper, or an ad in a specialized antique or auction paper. And don't forget the obvious: On any ad or flyer, check the auction date, the address, the phone numbers to call, the possible rain date, to be sure they're all correct. Does the ad say there will be food available? Should people bring their own chairs? Above all, check the driving directions, to determine if they are correct and clear for a person not familiar with the area.

If the auctioneer has a mailing list, find out if it has recently been updated. There is no point in wasting postage on five-year-old addresses, especially in these days of ever-upward mailing costs.

Now let's discuss some of the physical arrangements.

223

What kind of food will be served, and who will do it? Hot dogs seem to be standard fare, from small house sales to big estates. (They had a certain panache when they were sold at the Dunford estate, because the caterers had English accents.) Hot dogs are fine, except for people who are watching their weight, worrying about their salt consumption, or have never liked hot dogs. I am in all three categories, so I make a plea for offering some alternative. (Dunford also had either chicken or tuna salad on pita bread, and fresh fruit. I was delighted, and all of it sold well.) Having good food and drinks adds to the festive air, and keeps people on the premises so they will continue to bid.

Toilet facilities are important, and should include some way for washing hands; a garden hose with paper towels and trash cans nearby is a possibility. It's something that is frequently overlooked.

Ask about parking arrangements. Since people come and go, and often need room to load their purchases, it might be necessary to have someone in the parking area supervising traffic.

Unfortunately, security is a problem, even at neighborhood auctions. People come with big pocketbooks, or overalls with pockets, and are not above popping a few small items into them. So check on how tables full of small china and glassware will be protected, during both the presale exhibition and the auction itself.

### Easing the Confusion

Preparing for an auction, whether it's to be held at a home or in an auction gallery, requires a tremendous amount of tedious work: going through all the accumu-

225

lations of objects (and we all accumulate more than we plan to), listing, tagging, storing, transporting if necessary. At various points there is the possibility of loss through accidents and carelessness, and the opportunity for employees to be tempted. (For this reason, auctioneers have to be very careful whom they hire and how they supervise them. "You have to know your help," as one auctioneer told me.)

Ideally, you, as owner, should go through everything carefully, set up and keep your own records, give every item your own identification number, and keep a master list. If you can do this, you certainly should. In practice, however, few of us have the time for this task. The next

## Forgotten Treasures— Yours Or The Auctioneer's?

*Every auctioneer has his own little story about finding forgotten things stashed away in drawers and closets: rolls of cash, diamond rings, gold watches, lingerie, photographs, sets of false teeth. If you're handling someone else's property (a parent, for instance), your first task is to go through it carefully, opening all drawers and closets, especially closets that are parts of furniture. Rather than putting your hands in and risking splinters, use a flashlight to check out the dark corners where treasures might lie.*

*You may need to get a locksmith to open drawers and closets that are locked, but it could be worth it. One auctioneer recalls opening a desk drawer that had been locked, and finding in it a book that had been inscribed by Ernest Hemingway. (Under the terms of the contract with the consignor, he had the right to keep the book and auction it off—and he did.)*

best thing is to find out how the auctioneer will do it and what kind of record or receipts he will give you. Unless they supply you with duplicate records, you are dependent totally on the recordkeeping of the auction house—which, of course, is not the position you want to be in. If some or all of your goods are going to be in a catalog, you should also check you receipts against the catalog, to be sure you will be fully credited for everything of yours that is sold.

One possible source of confusion is nomenclature. You have a chest you inherited from your grandmother which for years was called Granny's bureau. (You know, when you were small, she would say, "Go upstairs and look in the top drawer of Granny's bureau.") But the auction house, following its own procedures, goes ahead to tag and list it as a chest of drawers. Which gets you to worrying. "What happened to my bureau?" You call and ask. Which gets them to worrying, until someone steps back a moment and untangles the problem. For your peace of mind and understanding, you should learn how the house lists its goods, what their numbering system is, and so on.

A final thought: You undoubtedly know some version of the old saying, "Where there's a will, there's a family feud" or "Where there's a will, there's an argument." One of my friends, who has a fine collection of antiques, has decided to leave instructions in his will that his estate be sold at auction. Each member of his family can buy what he or she wants at the auction. Then the net proceeds, after the auctioneer has been paid, will be divided among the family. He believes this scheme will prove to be a painless way of settling his estate.

And my last word: If you've decided to be famous, it may be all right—in fact it may be a good idea—to have your silver monogrammed, since the monogram could add to its potential worth. But if you're not planning to be famous, don't do it. It will detract from the value at auction.

# THE CLOSING BID: WINNERS AND LOSERS

In any game there are always winners and losers. The deciding factor is often a difference in degree of preparation, and the auction game is no exception. Here are some true tales of both, with brief morals. We'll concentrate on winners, but first the story of two winners who lost.

*The Case of Auction Fever:* In April 1980, Norton Simon, the industrialist and art collector, decided to bid for a fifteenth-century Flemish work, *Resurrection of Christ,* by the artist Dirk Bout. According to published reports, Mr. Simon understood only too well his love for early Renaissance art, and the danger of auction fever. So he decided not to attend the auction at Christie's in London, for fear he would succumb and try to buy the painting at any price. He admitted, "I was afraid I'd be

too subjective with it in front of me." His wife, the actress Jennifer Jones, went in his place, and saw the painting at the presale exhibition.

On the day of the auction, she bid until the price was up to $3 million; the major competitor was Britain's National Gallery. Apparently at that point Mr. Simon couldn't stand the possibility of losing the painting. He got on the transatlantic phone, took over the bidding, and finally triumphed at $4.5 million—a price that included the ten-percent buyer's premium and a value-added tax.

*Moral:* No one is immune to auction fever.

*The Case of the Oversized Painting:* After several perilous voyages to the polar regions to see and sketch icebergs from as close as he could get to them in a small boat, Frederick Church finished his masterpiece, *Icebergs,* in 1861. The huge picture—it measured five feet by nine feet—was sold to an English industrialist, Sir Edward Watkin, in 1863, and subsequently disappeared until it was rediscovered in Manchester, England, in

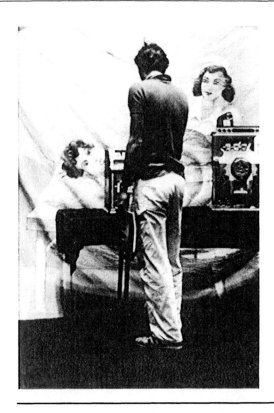

1979, in Sir Watkin's former residence, which had become a home for boys. It was sold at auction at Sotheby's New York, in October 1979 for $2.5 million, the highest price ever paid for an American painting, and at that time the highest price ever bid in the United States for any work of art. The buyer was an anonymous collector who subsequently donated the painting to the Dallas Museum of Fine Arts, Texas.

Later it was rumored that the anonymous donor was none other than a Texan, multimillionaire Lamar Hunt (of the famous Hunt family, known most recently for their attempt to corner the silver market). The reason for the donation? Some gossip has it that Mr. Hunt intended to keep the painting but discovered, too late, that it was too big for the wall on which he'd planned to hang it.

*Moral:* You've really got to measure the space available before you bid for something.

Now for the unqualified winners:

*The Case of the Henry Moore Lithograph:* Mr. and Mrs. E. L. collect prints, and very much wanted to add a Henry Moore to their collection. They went to a dealer who had a good selection at prices ranging from $600 to $1000, more than they wanted to spend. Then they went to a print auction at one of New York City's major houses, planning to bid on a George Grosz print.

"While we were there," says Mrs. E. L., "we noticed a Henry Moore and decided to bid on it too, since it was very good. We got it for $350, which we knew was a good price. Since then we've taken it to be professionally appraised; it's signed and is one of fifty, and it's worth about $1200."

*Moral:* It pays to shop around at dealers' shops to get some idea of values. then you can recognize a real find at an auction—and you'll know how much to bid.

*The Case of the Miscataloged Painting:* Mrs. R. B. works with her husband, who is an antique dealer, but she is also a painter, recently featured in an exhibition of women artists in New York City. When the R. B.s went to a presale exhibition at an estate on Long Island, she noticed a painting cataloged as the work of one Joseph Preffer, American artist. But Mrs. R. B. had studied with Joseph Presser and knew that when Mr. Presser signed his work, he used the old English *s* which looks like an *f*. She recognized the painting as the work of Joseph Presser, and worth more than the presale estimate.

"There was someone else there who also guessed the artist, and bid against me. But I won the bid at $200, and believe it's worth about $600—though I wouldn't part with it."

*Moral:* Catalogs are not infallible.

232

*The Case of the Jade Necklace:* Ms. D. D. A. has always been a devoted auction-goer. Her apartment in Chicago is furnished almost exclusively with items (furniture, dishes, decorative objects) bought at auctions around the country; most everything has appreciated tremendously in value since she bought it. Since her business involves traveling, she usually manages to go to a local auction when she's on the road. It was the last ten minutes of an auction in Los Angeles, and she decided to bid for a jade-look necklace.

"Even though my specialty is financial planning," she says, "I buy things that I like. I don't look for investments at auctions. I liked this necklace and I got it for $3, which seemed like a fair price. But when I got back to Chicago, just for the fun of it I took it to a jeweler I knew—and it turned out to be real jade, worth about $1500."

233

*Moral:* Buying what you like can pay off—although not often does it pay off as spectacularly as this necklace did.

*The Case of the Inelegant Bedroom Set:* Mr. and Mrs. L. M. were fairly regular customers of a large auction gallery in a New Jersey suburb, and often went to the regular Wednesday-night auctions. On this Wednesday there was a packed house, all eagerly waiting to bid on fine antiques and other elegant furniture from a well-known local estate; the presale estimates were in the thousand-dollar-and-up range. But the L. M.s had their eye on a used bedroom set, not an antique although it was finished in "antique grey."

"There was only one other person bidding on it," says Mrs. L. M., "because everybody else was waiting for the 'good stuff.' For $20 we got a tall dresser with six drawers, a wood-framed hanging mirror, a night table, a vanity which could also be used as a desk, and a stool upholstered in red velvet, that was meant to be used with the vanity. There weren't even any nicks in any of the pieces. Our teenager doesn't like the finish—but that's something that can be changed. It was a real buy."

*Moral:* There are often real buys in "odd pieces," those pieces that aren't part of the theme or the general level of most of the pieces in an auction.

*The Case of the Oriental Rug:* Attorney L. J. and his wife wanted an Oriental rug for their large Manhattan apartment. "We hung out at an auction house in our neighborhood," says Mr. L. J. "and got some idea of values. And we learned who the dealers were.

"One day we saw a beautiful ten-foot by seventeen-foot Oriental that was just what we wanted. The day it was auctioned we found ourselves bidding against the dealers. We kept bidding and they dropped out until there was only one left. Finally we made the successful bid.

"Afterward I approached the dealer who had lost and asked him what he thought the rug was worth.

" 'You've made a terrible mistake,' he said. 'Terrible, terrible. But I'll tell you what I'll do. I'll buy the rug from you right now and give what you paid for it.' "

The L. J.s have been enjoying the rug for several years now.

*Moral:* You can beat the dealers if you really want something, and have been following prices enough to know values. And if you bid just slightly above a dealer's last bid, you are buying at just a little above wholesale, since he would have to charge enough above his bid price to earn a profit.

*The Case of the Gold Buttons:* A New England auctioneer had taken some boxes of old uniforms as part of a one-day estate sale he was conducting. He wanted to sell the boxes quickly and get to the really valuable furniture, antiques, and so on. So he accepted a low bid of $40 for one box. Then, right before his eyes and the crowd, the bidder pulled a man's old blazer from the box, mentioned that the buttons were not brass, but gold, ripped them off and walked away, leaving the box behind. The auctioneer realized that the buttons would be sold for thousands of dollars.

*Moral:* It often pays to scrounge in box lots—and even auctioneers don't always know the value of their merchandise.

*The Case of the Antique Quilt:* Mrs. D. V. has been a collector of patchwork quilts since the days when they weren't so popular, or so expensive.

"I recently saw a full-sized patchwork quilt in a pyramid pattern that was most unusual," she says. "The pyramid was about 10,000 pieces, going all the way out to the edge. The only problem was that the whole border of the quilt was in terrible condition. However, I've been buying pieces of patchwork—'odd tops'—and keeping them, and I know a woman who is an expert in repairing old quilts.

"I bought the quilt for $40, gave her the tops, and for about $100 she repaired the quilt so beautifully you can't tell it's been touched.

"A dealer is photographing it for the cover of a book on Americana that he is working on; the quilt has earthy tones of green and brown in it. And I think the quilt is now worth about $1500 to $2000."

*Moral:* it pays to line up skilled craftspeople in advance

before buying at auction. Knowing that you can have something repaired or restored, and having some idea of what such repairs will cost, can help you get some rare finds.

The last word? What else but a good wish:
As you learn and follow the rules of the auction game, may you always be a winner!

# INDEX

Printed in the United States
62910LVS00004B/82